THE WAR OF THE SEXES

THE PROBLEMS & THE SOLUTIONS

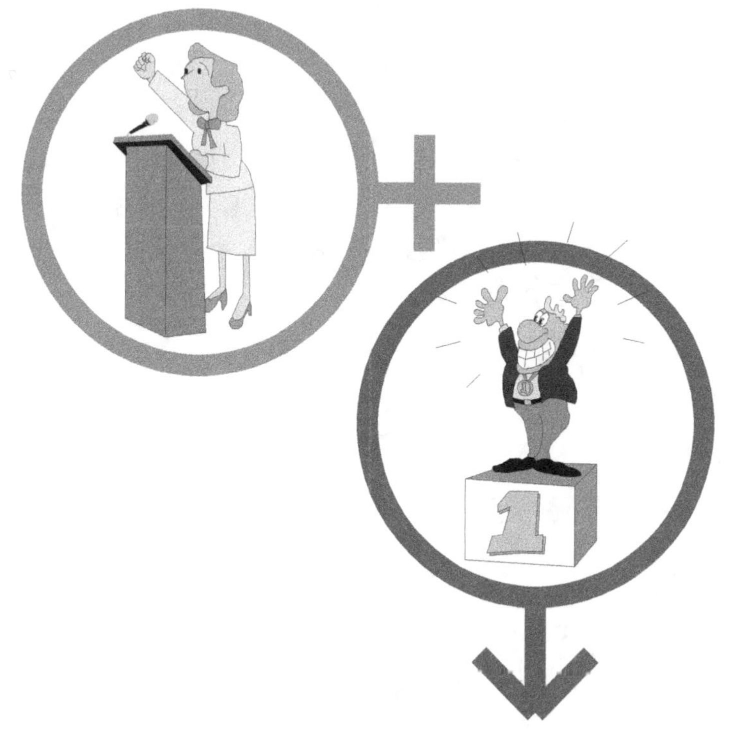

G. A. MOHR, PhD

THE WAR OF THE SEXES

THE PROBLEMS & THE SOLUTIONS

G. A. MOHR, PhD

G. A. Mohr, PhD

THE WAR OF THE SEXES
THE PROBLEMS & THE SOLUTIONS

Transworld Research & Innovation
9 Hampstead Drive
Hoppers Crossing VIC 3029
AUSTRALIA

ALSO BY G. A. MOHR

Finite Elements for Solids, Fluids, and Optimization

A Microcomputer Introduction to the Finite Element Method

The Pretentious Persuaders,
A Brief History & Science of Mass Persuasion

Curing Cancer & Heart Disease,
Proven Ways to Combat Aging, Atherosclerosis & Cancer

The Variant Virus, Introducing Secret Agent Simon Sinclair

The Doomsday Calculation, The End Of The Human Race

Heart Disease, Cancer, & Ageing:
Proven Neutraceutical & Lifestyle Solutions

2045: A Remote Town Survives Global Holocaust

The History & Psychology of Human Conflict

Elementary Thinking for the 21st Century

The 8-Week+ Program to Reverse Cardiovascular Disease

The Scientific MBA

Mohr's Law of Hierarchies

The DIY Cardiovascular Cure

ALSO WITH R.S. MOHR/RICHARD SINCLAIR & P.E. MOHR/EDWIN FEAR

The Evolving Universe: Relativity, Redshift and Life from Space

World Religions: The History, Psychology, Issues & Truth

World War 3, When & How Will It End?

The Brainwashed, From Consumer Zombies to Islamic Jihad

Human Intelligence, Learning & Behaviour

The Psychology of Hope

New Theories of The Universe, Evolution, and Relativity

The Population Explosion

Brainwashed Zombies: Religious, Political & Consumer
Persuasion

World Religions: From Animism to Mohronism

TABLE OF CONTENTS

PREFACE

Friedrich Engels thought original pairing societies were matrilineal, if not matriarchal, because the main point of production was in the household (Tong, 1998).

The Agricultural Revolution, and then the Industrial Revolution, however, put most production in the hands of men.

Over two hundred years ago the seeds of the feminist movement were sown in Europe:

A king is always a king – and a woman always a woman:
his authority and her sex ever stand
between them and rational discourse.
Mary Wollstonecraft, mother of Mary Shelley,
A Vindication of the Rights of Woman (1792).

In the USA the First Women's Rights Convention was held in New York in 1848 and declared that all men and women are created equal.

Doubtless the word 'created' is used with God in mind but, in the rampant and corrupt capitalism that has the real power in most of the world now, neither men or women are born equal, far from it. On the contrary, a few are born rich and the rest are not.

As noted in Chapter One, the more rampant modern feminist movement was launched by such writers as de Beauvoir and Greer. Women already having gained 'the vote', in the West at least, they were given, in principle at least, equal pay for equal work.

In part because of feminism, however, in the decadent West 50% of marriages now end in divorce.

What men and women need, therefore, is not to stand in opposition, but to communicate and thus cooperate in partnership, making the best possible use of the slightly differing physical, emotional, sociological and perhaps intellectual differences between men and women.

Thus, having discussed the feminist movement and The War of the Sexes in the first two chapters, I discuss the differences between the sexes in Chapters 3 to 7.

In Chapters 8 to 13 the weaknesses of modern women in our ever more morally and financially bankrupt societies are discussed.

In Chapters 14 to 18 the way in which women are beginning to take over the workforce at the expense of men is discussed, whilst in Chapter 19 the overall decay of Western Civilization is lamented.

Finally, in Chapters 20 to 25 an attempt is made to make some constructive suggestions to remedy some of the problems posed by feminism and high divorce rates.

Thus it is suggested that marital-type relationships should always be a carefully chosen and communicative and constructive partnership between compatible, like-minded people.

In Chapters 22 and 24 it is suggested that those who have children should, bearing in mind the present greatly excessive human population which is rapidly polluting and depleting the earth, have only one or two children (Mohr, 2012c). Then it is noted that this generally results in smarter children, and Chapter 24 is devoted to discussing how to make one's children smarter from almost day 1.

The bottom line is that when a couple has children a family is formed. Families are a 'blood line' thing and, to that extent, have an unbreakable bond. Thus, for the sake of their children parents should not separate if it is at all avoidable.

The parents may have, of course, different skills, different backgrounds, different educations, different types of job, different interests and so forth.

That they are of different sex, however, is the very fundamental reason for them 'shacking up' together and being able to have children, and living as a family is the fundamental way of life Homo sapiens has evolved with.

Unfortunately, outside influences contribute a great deal to the current high divorce rates, these including rampant consumerism that reduces us to *consumer zombies*, incompetent government and economic management, and corrupt capitalism (Mohr, 2012a; Mohr & Fear, 2016; Mohr et al., 2018a). As a result of such factors the real standard of living in the West had been declining for decades, despite the usual obfuscation of politicians and bureaucrats that assures us otherwise. One example of this is that, not long ago, mothers did not have to work, whereas most now have to, despite having little cash left over after paying the high costs of day care for their children, the latter form of imprisonment being yet another decline in living standards, and a major one at that.

Thus the War of the Sexes is, of course, a sociological problem, but one which arises not only from the aspirational writings of feminists, but also from the decadence of many modern societies and the incompetence of the leaders of these societies, be they their governments, religious leaders, or leaders of pressure groups such as the feminist movement.

There is no easy solution, therefore, but the author hopes that many a reader perplexed or just intrigued by the War of the Sexes will find useful ideas in this book that may be of help in their own lives.

Finally, thanks again to the staff at Amazon Kindle for their highly efficient publishing system.

Geoff Mohr, 2018

DISCLAIMER

In this book the author seeks to restore a little balance to the War of the Sexes. This cannot be done without firing an occasional broadside at 'broads.'

To help give balance many comments by women writers such as Germaine Greer are included in the book.

Some of the content is based on my past experience, some of it a little dated now (I was married on 10/1/70, for example). That long experience and a life spent studiously have helped me devote a good deal of the book to making constructive suggestions, especially in the later chapters, which I hope are helpful to many readers.

To add a final bit of balance, however, I should note that most of we men admire women for their demanding mothering role, one which forces them to be relatively sensible. Men, however, once humans formed tribes, were able to become complete idiots playing competitive games and fighting wars. They still do!

Indeed, it is this tribalism that has been the cause of a great many of man's problems, a current example being the almost global problems posed by Muslim extremists.

The War of the Sexes also has a tribal aspect, leading to 50% divorce rates in the decadent West when, in fact, it is family groupings that Homo sapiens evolved with. In other words, this is a serious breakdown in our society which we should do everything in our power to prevent, and this is the main aim of this book.

Finally, I should like to note that many years ago in both Australia and New Zealand a rare and lonely female engineering student came to me, not the HOD, talking of quitting the course. I told them to stick it out and they did, though one then went on to do Medicine.

Chapter 1

THE FEMINIST MOVEMENT: WOE TO MEN

We hold these truths to be self-evident,
that all men and women are created equal.
Elizabeth Cady Stanton, *Declaration of Sentiments,*
First Women's Rights Convention, Seneca, New York, 1848.

Join the union girls, and together say Equal Pay for Equal Work.
Susan B. Anthony, speech in Chicago, Illinois July 10, 1858.

You can see the female eunuch the world over . . .
Wherever you see nail varnish, lipstick, brassieres, and high heels,
The Eunuch has set up her camp.
Germaine Greer, *The Female Eunuch,*
Forward to the 20th anniversary edition.

Introduction

The symbols for male and female shown with altered orientation on the cover derive from the astrological symbols for the planets Mars and Venus, themselves respectively named after the Roman god of war and the Roman goddess of cultivated fields and gardens (later associated with Aphrodite, daughter of Zeus and goddess of sexual love and beauty).

Placing the female symbol on top, as well as the altered orientation given to the symbols, is meant to illustrate the subtitle 'Women Are Getting On Top' of a previous edition of this book and thus that the feminist movement has in recent decades had a considerable impact (Mohr, 2012d).

The women's suffrage movement

The roots of the feminist movement go back deep into history, no doubt, for example, women occasionally rising to leadership of a country, perhaps when there was no male heir available to take on the role.

The grass roots of the widespread feminism we see still growing slowly today, however, probably lay in Europe in the 19th century when the women's suffrage movement helped women to be given equal voting rights in several countries.

In 1881, the Isle of Man gave women who owned property the right to vote, whilst the British colonies of New Zealand and South Australia granted all women the right to vote in 1893 and 1895 respectively, South Australia also allowing women to stand for election.

Western Australia gave women the vote in a referendum in 1900, and in state and federal elections in 1901. In 1902 women in Australia's other four colonies were granted the vote when the colonies federated to become the Commonwealth of Australia.

Subsequently, many other countries gave women voting rights, for example Finland in 1907, Norway in 1913, Denmark in 1915, the Soviet Union and Canada in 1917, Britain in 1918 (over 30) and 1928 (over 21), Germany and Poland in 1918, Austria and the Netherlands in 1919, the USA in 1920, Spain in 1933, France in 1944 and Italy in 1946.

The Feminine Liberation movement

The 'Feminine Liberation' movement, on the other hand, began to take off after World War Two, perhaps in part because of the major part women played in that war, particularly in England as nurses and in the Home Guard.

A principal cause of development of the feminist movement was the economic need for more women to work to pay increasingly high costs of living, in particular higher rents and mortgages as housing prices escalated.

Thus increasingly rampant capitalism in the West, despite the economic bullshit or *econobabble* that cons us into thinking we've never had it so good, has gradually reduced our real standard of living.

One of the books that helped inspire 'Fem Lib' was Simone de Beauvoir's *Le Deuxieme Sex* (1949) which appeared translated into English as *The Second Sex* in 1953.

Fem Lib really began to have an impact by the 1970s, however, in part thanks to the Germaine Greer's *The Female Eunuch* (1970), Greer having been something of a fan of de Beauvoir.

Now, of course, it seems an unstoppable force, just one of many factors changing human society.

Indeed, a recent book with a Foreword by Germaine Greer is entitled: *Female Erasure: What You Need To Know About Gender Politics' War on Women, the Female Sex and Human Rights* suggests that the title of this book is, indeed, justified and appropriate (Barret, 2016).

For the most part, I contend, things are getting worse as our grossly overpopulated human population becomes more and more decadent. Indeed, I contend that we are in *reverse evolution* (Mohr, 2012a; Mohr & Fear, 2016; Mohr et al., 2018a), one key result of which is that our intelligence is decreasing.

One reason for this is our growing insistence that all men (and women) are 'equal' (in all respects, presumably), whereas all human history contradicts this absurd assertion. Indeed, it was only through the inspiration and efforts of exceptional people that we invented fire, writing, electricity, antibiotics, and so forth.

Now, however, a grossly unfair society in which most of us are supposedly 'equal slaves' to a very few disgustingly greedy and rich capitalist 'pigs' demands that both husband and wife must work increasingly longer hours with fewer and fewer benefits to pay the increasingly expensive and long-drawn out mortgage on their house.

In this scenario, of course, feminine liberation has failed as more and more women, rather than stick to the admirable task of caring for a household and the family in it, have been able to also become slaves to 'big biz' themselves.

Sure, women can now aspire to become capitalist pigs also, but, of course, only a very few will succeed, and at the expense of their fellow women, of course.

Equal pay

One of the key demands of Feb Lib has always been equal pay for equal work. That sounds fair to me.

This has to some extent come about though there is still some distance to go. In particular, complaints about the 'glass ceiling' that is supposed to discriminate against women rising up through hierarchical management structures continue. Progress has been made in that area too, however, and, no doubt, it will continue.

Overall, however, as subtitle of this book suggests, it seems to me that women are beginning to not just catch up with men, but get ahead. Often, for example, a woman can take years out of the workforce to have a child or two, and then return to it older and wiser, with the higher and somewhat protected status of being a mother. They usually return with no loss of seniority in the workplace, and indeed are often able to use their now greater age as a bargaining tool in seeking advancement.

In contrast, in those extra years in the workforce, men have often tired of their job, perhaps because of lack of promotion or even simply change in the job. Indeed, in those extra years they and their bosses have had reciprocal rights to tire of each other, often with disastrous results for the long-suffering workers.

In other words, women never had it so bad at all really, and enjoyed a somewhat privileged position in society as mothers and carers.

Now, however, they can have the best of both worlds, that is, they can concentrate on family life, as countless single mothers with young children are forced to do, or they can put their children in day care and concentrate more upon their careers.

Sexual jealousy

Earlier feminist authors such as Simone de Beauvoir and Germaine Greer were somewhat obsessed with sex, that is the act(s) of sex, to say the least and, regrettably, their writings never rise to any great intellectual level.

One major issue they raise is that of female orgasm and de Beauvoir opines that the self-stimulation of the clitoris perpetuates juvenile independence whilst sexual intercourse is a reminder of childbearing and economic dependence on a male (Kipnis, 2007).

As for going it alone with self-stimulation of the vagina, Greer considers "digital massage" to be "pompous and deliberate" and says that women should demand more than just orgasm, that they should demand ecstasy (Greer, 1970).

Myself I think this is a bit out of place and many a keen sports fan, for example, might have a better chance of feeling ecstasy when their team has a big win or, better still, wins a grand final or Olympic gold medal. At least there's something to show for it rather than smelly muck etcetera.

Attacks on men

Very few women can sit without something in their hands to work on; all men sit for hours relaxing. Women cannot go out without something to carry; men keep their hands free and move about unburdened as much as possible.
Women are busy; men are idle.
Germaine Greer, *The Whole Woman* (1999).

The last line of this quotation is somewhat objectionable, to say the least, as is the originally sex-obsessed moron that wrote it. All history disproves it.

As one popular song of the seventies put it: "Man made the car - -, man made the plane - -" and so on. In fact, man made just about everything.

Men, indeed, were far from lazy. While their women were busy sitting on the backsides and yakking, as they still do a great deal, of course, the men were out hunting, or regrettably, fighting wars. The latter is not lazy really, but undoubtedly stupid.

And there is no doubt that humans are stupid in excess, and all history proves it. My ninth law is that 'Murphy is God' because in human history things almost always go wrong sooner or later and, for example, penicillin was discovered by accident. In other words, those clever things that the very few really clever people amongst us invented were very much the exception, not the rule. That nearly all of those clever inventors were men was in part owing to the wider spread of the Gaussian Distribution of human IQ, a point I return to in Chapter 5.

Women taking over

I recall my wife (now ex-wife) telling me assertively in my Cambridge days:

Children under three can't count to three.

Hogwash from a Greer-loving woman with an IQ of circa 90 in her prime when she passed only 'unfailable unless you didn't speak much English' English Literature at Matriculation exams in Melbourne. So she became a kindergarten teacher, and after a 13-year break during which she was happy to see me "used up" and backstab me everywhere, including at work, she helped destroy my promising academic career.

At that point trying to build a career had involved massive sacrifice and toils and I had not yet made any profit to speak of at all. Timing her virtual assassination of me well, she was able to advance her career, becoming boss of a Long Day Care Centre, something she enjoyed, being "boss of 12 people".

As my dying mother put it: *"She has to be the boss."*

True. Ambitious women and Hitler have a lot in common as many men will tell you.

For example: I heard on ABC news at 7 AM one morning that an Australian woman was on trial in Canada for, in 2010, murdering her two sons because of a "difficult divorce." Had they been daughters, of course, I very much doubt if she would have killed them. More important, however, is that the proportion of crimes committed by women is gradually increasing.

It often seems to me that women prefer the company of other women, or even dogs, which they can boss around like surrogate children, and husbands are caught by seduction and used as slaves, as the title of this book suggests. They own his body and soul, his cheque book, etcetera, and his only purpose is to provide children and play protector and hunter-gatherer and bring home the bacon while they have children.

Indeed, while emasculating men, women are 'masculating' themselves so that they "wear the pants," and that is exactly what most of them now do, along with business suits that are a modified version of traditional men's suits, but much tighter to show off their figure, a catastrophic situation if they are much overweight.

So it is that some women, trying to be more masculine or 'butch', go to strip clubs to "be like a man" (Levy, 2005).

Indeed, some women also like porn such as "stick movies" as my ex-wife called what I presume she and her women friends watched on dirty weekends away, leaving the children with granny.

Western Civilization Falling Apart

Make no mistake, Western civilization is falling apart.

Decadence has been increasing slowly for a few hundred years at least, perhaps with the breaking away of England and Germany from the dominance of the strict but corrupt and hypocritical Catholic Church.

The process no doubt accelerated with the onset of the Industrial Revolution that saw the birth of rampant capitalism and exploitation of the workers who worked day and night to produce the new products and then spend their meager wages buying the rubbish produced en masse.

Then along came advertising, which in the USA in the early 20th Century began to employ psychologists to brainwash consumers (Eagly & Chaiken, 1993), most of whom, of course, were women:

> *We seem to have misplaced the sense of values which made this a great nation. Self-indulgence and the principle of pleasure before duty on a vast and growing scale have become a phenomenon of the adult world.*
> *These are warning symptoms of the decadence disease which has contributed to the decay*
> *of so many civilizations throughout history.*
> (Packard, 1963, quoting "some official").

Thus, our societies are becoming meaner, nastier and more violent at an alarming rate. Violence is on the increase everywhere to the point that many people don't feel safe on the streets at night and, of course, there is no shortage of street crime during the day as well.

Experiments with rats show that when they are housed beyond a certain population density they begin to fight each other. Evidently, humans do the same and we are now accustomed to associating crime and violence with big cities like Chicago and New York.

Increasing numbers of us are addicted to booze, illegal so-called 'party drugs,' as well as prescription drugs like Valium for anxiety, Ritalin for ADHD, and lithium for bipolar disorder (formerly called manic depression).

With divorce rates around 50% we are living less safely in this respect at least than our Neanderthal ancestors did. Childhood is miserable enough at times but family breakups often make it much more so for far too many children.

Women loose tolerance of the fact that men, especially when younger, can drink far more booze than they. They also fear violence from men though they are more often than not at least, the instigators by way of a what police call a 'verbal assault.' Try that on the footy field and, predictably, you can 'get an opponent in' so that they take a shot at you and risk being 'rubbed out' for a few weeks by the umpires.

In marriage, as well as in courtship, there is little or no meaningful communication. If you eavesdrop on a couple that has been married for a decade or two you will find the dialogue at all times entirely trivial, for example: "Do we need milk?," in modern times this being said as often as not over a mobile phone while one partner is in the supermarket.

Indeed, with the War of the Sexes heating up and women taking over in management, politics, and education, and running the countless industries that target women consumers, the future is bleak indeed for our decadent society.

Indeed, you can see the writing on the walls, that is, the graffiti that covers much of our miserable megacities, a sure sign that young men with nothing better to do are regressing back to grunting cave men once again.

This is, indeed, something of a reversal in roles. Once it was probably troglodyte women who did the cave painting, perhaps to teach children, while the men were out hunting. Now, as manufacturing industry winds down inexorably in most countries except a few in Asia, more and more men are out of work whereas new, 'softer' jobs for women continue to be created, for example in childcare centres.

Conclusions

Laura Kipnis opines that *feminism* and *femininity* are mutually exclusive, which may be somewhat true at least.

She writes on breast implants:

More irony: here are so-called modern women slicing and dicing body parts to achieve a feminine ideal – and even if "freely chosen" [as distinct from widespread genital mutilation in some societies], *the cut of the knife is just as sharp as back in the village. You hear a lot of talk about "assertiveness" in women's culture today, except your hear it from women shopping for baby-doll outfits, or getting Brazilian bikini waxes, or double D-cup breast implants. "I **like** feeling like a woman," she'll assert (or demur). If there's a backlash against feminism, most of those carrying it out these days are women, just trying to "feel like women."*

This statement suggests that women, rather than trying to be feminine, should concentrate their efforts on winning the War of the Sexes.

Chapter 2

HOW MEN ARE CAPTURED

A good part - and definitely the most fun part –
of being a feminist is about frightening men.
Julie Burchill, *Time Out* (London, 16 Nov. 1989).

Beautiful thoughts, and beautiful women never last.
Charles Bukowski, *The Dirty Old Man* (1969).

Women's Liberation is just a lot of foolishness. It's the men who
are discriminated against. They can't bear children.
And no one's likely to do anything about that.
Golda Meir, quoted in: *Newsweek* (New York, 23 Oct. 1972).

The War of the Sexes

As noted in Chapter 1, in large part the modern feminist movement was based on jealousy, jealousy about feeling inferior because the role of full-time housewife and carer was seen as being lower on the social scale than that of breadwinner.

There was, of course, also an economic factor, that of women wanting to earn their own money rather than rely on handouts from hubby. As noted in Chapter 1, the economic factor became more imperative with the rise and rise of excessive and corrupt capitalism in the far from free 'Free West' where it became increasingly necessary for both husband and wife to work to pay increasingly high rents and mortgages.

With the advent of Germaine Greer's *The Female Eunuch*, however, sexual equality also became a significant issue for the feminist movement. A counter argument might have been, however, that men could feel hard done by because they cannot bear children. In other words, there are, in fact, very considerable differences between men and women, both physically, and mentally, an issue discussed further in the next Chapter.

Kipnis (2007) brings some balance to the sex issue by noting that recent studies found that up to 58 percent of women consistently fail to have orgasms and that this arouses some jealousy amongst women but that, on the other hand, many women may prefer not to feel under some pressure to achieve sexual climax like "some kind of performing seal."

The battle for the right of women to vote, of course, has long been won, and the battle for equal pay for equal work is almost won. The battle for women to break through the 'glass ceiling' in organizational management hierarchies, however, has some way to go.

In other words, with many battles now won, the *War of the Sexes* continues and, to this author, it looks like the women are edging ahead.

How women catch men

Women catch their man-slave with a range of artifices including:

> **Seduction.**

Young girls today show it off like never before, that is, some cleavage, tight pants etcetera. The hair and makeup are doted over but you will be treated like a fool spending time with a high-class prostitute and the conversations will always be as mindless, but perhaps more mundane than phone sex chat lines. But the *implications* will always be laid on thick and the young, inexperienced fool high on testosterone is looking for heterosexual experience at last.

In large part the girl's motivation is keeping up with the yak fests in her circle of girlfriends. In these her experiences with men will be described in graphic detail, just as Anne Lister described her many lesbian experiences in her 4 million words of coded diaries some 300 years ago in England (Anne Lister's history is briefly given in the 'Lesbians' section of Chapter 12).

> **Dating.**

Dating is a key part of the procedure for catching a mate. First you must meet them at school or at work, as neighbours, or at dances, but increasingly these days on the Internet,

The latter is real desperado stuff, especially when the woman is circa 30, childless and in danger of being left on the shelf. Then, of course, if the date is in a noisy, dark nightclub, and lots of grog and perhaps other drugs are had, then the male victim has little idea of what he's getting into. Alcohol, being a tranquillizer, reduces inhibitions, which I summarize by the table:

Table 2.1. The effects of different blood alcohol levels.

State	# drinks	BAL	Effects
R	1-3	0 - .03%	**R**elaxed
U	3-5	.03 - 0.05%	**U**ninhibited
B	5-12	.05 - .10%	**B**abbling
B	12-18	.10 - .15%	**B**oozed
I	18-24	.15 - .20%	**I**ncoherent
S	25-35	.25 - .35%	**S**leeping
H	35	.35% to ?	**H**eaven (for keeps!)

The table unrealistically assumes you've consumed the stated number of drinks in about an hour. It takes about an hour to metabolize one standard drink (SD), that is, 100 ml of wine or 250 ml of full strength beer. Table 2.1 does, however, make the point, but note that the higher levels of consumption mentioned might relate to the physical (not mental!) capacity of an experienced drinker and probably a large, young, fit and well-muscled male.

In this scenario, the male joke about certain alcoholic drinks being a "leg opener" backfires and the man becomes the victim of the woman's ambitions for children and a man-slave to provide them.

Once in a relatively exclusive little bar in one of Melbourne's poshest suburbs a 'lady' friend said after I'd bought her a brandy (she ordered a Cognac but didn't know the difference, of course):

> *It must be annoying to have to do that*
> [act as unpaid drink waiter, i.e. man-slave]
> *but there must be some compensations.*

> ➢ **Dating agencies and the Internet.**

Agencies that find lonely people a prospective partner of the opposite sex have been around for a century or so.

In the last decade or two phone chat services have taken over and these are advertised heavily on late night TV, as are 'dirty talk' phone services as well.

More recently, Internet dating services have appeared, allowing lonely people to post written biographical information and photos of themselves for the entire world to see in the hope of finding at least one person who might take an interest in meeting them face to face.

More rarely, but more amusing perhaps, are speed dating events run occasionally at pubs and clubs. In these farces one is given just a minute or two to chat to a series of members of the opposite sex and then asked to choose one's favourite choice.

➢ **Lying**

Women are accomplished liars. For example, one woman caught me by lying about her age (by 9 years) in the gloom of the first mature age singles dance I attended.

She was, like most women, a chronic liar, saying, for example, "You have to lie to get jobs." She did and I didn't after being crucified academically with my wife playing the role of Judas and backstabbing me at every opportunity.

Another woman had been sacked from her position as chairperson of a charity organization. Somehow related to this, I suspect she had been committed for perhaps only a short while to a psychiatric institution.

Thus, she responded to a house-sharing ad by turning up in a white uniform saying she was a "diet consultant at Melbourne {psychiatric] Clinic," a rather hilarious situation that suggested she might, indeed, have been a bit nutty.

My ex-wife too was a psychopathic liar whose pathology also included convective hysteria, bossiness, and bullying, all of which made my life quite miserable, to say the least. Worse still, her lying and backstabbing always reached the ears of my employers, an impossible situation that eventually impacted and destroyed my University career with the help of two literally criminally bent halfwit HODs in succession.

As for a woman's sexual history: that is hard to ascertain. Some act like virgins, whereas the man's past must be known in detail, another example of the hypocrisy of which women are highly capable and often guilty.

➢ **House and flat sharing.**

In modern times, thanks to the curse of high rents but also to our much less strict morals in our decaying and decadent societies, it is common for two or more people to share a flat or house. Especially when there are more than two people cohabiting, more often than not there will be a mix of sexes.

Living in such close proximity to a member of the opposite sex, for example perhaps sitting on the same couch to watch TV, makes greater intimacy and sexual relations a quite likely outcome in the fullness of time, especially, of course, if both parties are 'single.'

After a disastrous marriage breakup the author more than once advertised a large spare room in a large house and found many women more than happy to try living with him. In some cases they were clearly looking for a partner as soon became obvious and, indeed, this is nowadays a common way in which men and women 'hook up.'

> **Getting pregnant.**

I recall a neighbour around the corner from me in 2010 saying, out of the blue it seemed to me,

That's how they [women] *catch you* [by getting pregnant].

Indeed, this had happened to him and to his son who had found himself with 2 children renting a house (not far from granny of course) and running two cars (of course, the wife had to have a flashy SUV). None of this could the young wharfie man really afford but he had been caught well and truly because he met a young girl at a dance in one of Melbourne's better suburbs, Sandringham.

Indeed, he had only grown up in neighbouring Cheltenham because his wharfie father had been laid off in a massive downsizing of the docks labour force, his retrenchment package allowing him to afford a house in Cheltenham, a 'middle of the road' suburb price-wise.

This man was too young to be saddled with Zorba's "full catastrophe," just as I had been many years earlier when I married a woman from the wrong side of the tracks in terms of background, her father having been a chronic alcoholic pastry cook, mine one of the men who split the atom in Cambridge in 1931.

➢ **Forgetting to take The Pill.**

One way to get pregnant, other than by carelessness etc., is to be on The (contraceptive) Pill and then forget to take it.

Myself, I was always suspicious when my wife, having gone back to study a postgraduate course after seeing me complete one early in the marriage, got pregnant in the middle of it.

I suspected that, a couple around the corner who we were friendly with having split up, she was nervous that I might dump her too and just neglected to take the pill once too often. In any event she never spoke of the fact that, in all likelihood, she should not have got pregnant while taking the pill. This would have been a normal conversation to have, leaving me suspicious to this day.

In any event, we had not saved any money and I had just borrowed money to pay for about half of a new car, having tired of the usual used car hassles.

The bottom line is that, she being the person risking pregnancy, a woman should do everything possible to prevent pregnancy and, if in doubt, avoid the breeding act at all costs, something which 2 women in the few years after my divorce did not bother about and got pregnant.

Both were 30 – 35 and wanting a child anyway and I an unthinking, boozing down-and-out still a bit used to the silly sex habit of marriage (a bad one).

Fortunately, one had a miscarriage. In the other case, on hearing that the child might be "slightly retarded" and consulting experts to find that this actually was quite significant retardation, I rang the woman (then overseas) and talked her into an abortion at 5 months which she found a little emotionally distressing saying (over the phone): "it looked like a child" or some such.

I never saw her again though a friend visited and said: "She still loves you." BS. In my down and out condition she had sometimes been quite rude in looking down on me.

➢ **Really desperate women**

An example of what really desperate women will do when 'love struck' by some movie or sports star is given in Marlon Brando's memoirs (Brando & Lindsey, 1994).

In the episode in question Brando was at home in bed in the middle of the night with a lady friend, of whom he had many in his spectacular career. Brando awoke to see a woman standing at the end of the bed and asked her why she was there. The deranged woman insisted that he must have seen her at the bus stop the previous afternoon.

Brando turned to face his lady friend to explain that he had never seen the strange woman before in his life. At that point the intruder removed her clothes and hopped naked into Brando's bed.

Brando pushed her out of the bed but, unable to persuade her to leave, called the police who took her off the property.

He went back to sleep for a while only to awake to again find the deranged woman back in his bedroom.

She said angrily: "Haven't you got rid of her yet?"

This time the police said they had more pressing things to do than take woman out of Brando's house but he bluffed the strange woman into believing the police were on their way again and that he would press charges and she would go to jail for a year.

The woman left and he never saw her again, but on another occasion he found a strange woman in his bathroom, whilst on several other occasions strange women appeared at his doorstep.

Many other male celebrities have suffered such intrusions by women, for example ex AFL footballer Sam Newman when he had become a star of Channel 9 Australia's 'The Footy Show.'

Worse still, these days, of course, is the willingness of desperate, divorced and lonely women to move in and live with and 'catch' men and that happened to me more than once when I advertised a spare room.

➢ **Corralling a man.**

An example, of this, one woman trying to catch me scolded me for looking at another woman while we were drinking at the front bar of Melbourne's famous 'Espy' hotel. I had little choice, we were sitting on bar stools facing along the length of the bar and I could not see much else but the single bar maid on duty at the off-peak time in question.

That you are not allowed to talk to other women socially, of course, goes without saying. In other words, you are cut-off and become an isolated male slave/eunuch.

➢ **Fighting off the opposition.**

I recall one 'lady' friend visiting my house and violently attacking a woman renting a room in it because she thought she was showing too much of her breasts. She had her pinned to the floor and was tearing her hair out. I called the police and told her to leave ASAP because they were coming. They came but, unlike a woman, I did not dob her in as that would have got her into a lot of trouble.

A lady friend, will, of course, always be quick to run down other women verbally should she perceive them as any sort of a threat to your attention to her. Indeed, they can often be highly disparaging and downright rude in this context.

➢ **Getting emotional.**

Turning on the tears, of course, largely an act sometimes, can win a woman sympathy very quickly indeed and help con a man into taking pity on her and doing as she wants.

One can, of course, relieve one's emotions with grog.

I recall a nurse at one of my eldest brother's undergraduate student parties sleeping off half a bottle of Scotch on the lawn. No doubt she was upset at being left on the shelf somewhat and seeking attention, however subconsciously.

My then wife did the same thing at a party in Auckland when I talked to 2 other women (she was a bit of a retard who could not talk to me beyond one-liners which I equate to the grunts of animals).

I drove her home, returned, and, despite having a "communication problem" according to my insane wife, I was last man standing to talk to the hostess and console her about grief over her father's death, the reason why she had returned to Auckland and bought a nice house, despite her husband not having a job, but who cares about him – he was just the man-slave or, too all intents and purposes, the male eunuch.

> **Love.**

Love is the most misused word in every language. People 'love' their spouse, their dog, their children, their football team, chocolate, nice weather, a favourite holiday spot, nice-looking cars, and so on ad infinitum. In other words they love almost everything, in some way and to some extent at least.

As meaningless as it is, the 'love card' is played sooner or later as a means of persuading a person to become a live-in partner in life.

Indeed, Love is one of the world's biggest industries, providing us with countless books, movies, TV sitcoms, dating agencies and other businesses such as tourism.

As I point out in three recent books (Mohr, 2012a; Mohr & Fear, 2016; Mohr et al., 2018a), human society has always been largely controlled by the bullshit of religious nutters, raving and often warmongering rulers, and in modern times by a plethora of advertising.

All the raving about Love is just another part of that bullshit.

I told my wife to be that I did not believe in love.

I still don't, the world 'love' being thoughtlessly used in dozens of contexts ranging from 'loving' a particular food or drink, sport, TV series or movie – indeed to the point at which the word 'love' is largely meaningless, or at best means 'like'.

I believe instead that a young man might get 'the hots' for a girl, that is, become infatuated with her and imprint her into his small 'family circle' as an infant does the familiar faces of parents it sees every day.

If, as a result, their relationship lasts any significant amount of time, then it is very likely that at least one of the couple will become habituated to the other person. In some cases people marry and live together until parted by death and, of course, in such cases their relationship is a very strong habit indeed, involving as it does a good deal of role play and life-sharing. I would contend, however, that it is more role play and habit than love.

> **Training the man and the dog.**

Whenever I see a young woman taking her boyfriend and dog for a walk I say to myself (silently):

"She's training him."

And she is doing just that. She is training the young, gullible sucker who is brainwashed by our culture to put women on a pedestal of some sort.

She is giving him obedience training, as she is the dog, which comes higher in the pecking order and is more important than he is. He is the male eunuch, merely a tool by which she has, or will, achieve her ultimate goal in life, her biological purpose, having children.

So important is this goal, the ancient Greeks thought, that the word hysteria originally meant in ancient Greek 'without a womb', and was applied to childless women who, even so long before Freud and Jung, it was presumed were crazy as a result. Indeed, I have met more than one woman completely insane, and sadly so, because they had been deserted by a (male) partner of some years and left 'on the shelf' at 30+, in my youth considered the age at which women who had not caught a man were in danger of never doing so, having lost their looks somewhat.

> **Other connivances**

Other elements of women's various machinations, which are many, include persuading you into doing things for them to the point at which it becomes a habit (i.e. you have been obedience trained),

This persuasiveness of women usually wins out in the end to the point at which the man is virtually a slave, just one of her menagerie and perhaps below the dog or cat in her order of importance. Indeed, when a woman is frightened or threatened she will all too quickly call upon her man-slave to support and protect her and, no doubt, such influences have played a part in mankind's disastrous and never ending history of war.

The male eunuch

In jest we call a man's genitals "the family jewels."

There is some truth in this, for, as wedding vows used to attest, when a man marries he gives his all to the woman.

This is true. She owns the man in every part – all his possessions, including his penis which is the tool by which she gets children, as the maternal instinct tells her too.

That is why the bastard title of this book was at one early stage *The Male Eunuch*. Indeed, according to Greer (1970), women should demand ecstasy, not just orgasm, from the male, but, like Simone de Beauvoir before her, felt that manual assistance was "pompous and deliberate."

Myself, I think women demand too much, having much in common with the babies they fret over in that regard.

Conclusions

Some bottom lines emerge at this early stage, for example:

➢ In the corrupt and decaying West women are taking over. One lady friend put it thus:

"Women are taking over the world."

She belonged to International Training in Communication (ITC), formerly known as Toastmistresses International, where, no doubt, they hatched their plans for dominance over men over a few drinks, just like men used to do but now more and more of them are "house husbands" looking after the children, that is, the tables are turning.

➢ Corrupt capitalism is encouraging Western decline so whilst the econobabble tells us we've never had it so good, in fact house prices just exploded, along with interest rates, forcing both husbands and wives to work to pay the rent or mortgage. All too often now, middle-aged men are first to be laid off during economic crises, becoming casualties in a sick, corrupt society.

➢ In contrast, China's socialist central committee government allows capitalism in a tightly regulated economy with a pegged exchange rate, and as always, capitalists like using cheap, if not slave labour. Notably, China's 1-child policy has worked well and been an example of reducing the war of the sexes, or at least controlling it.

➢ Women are incredibly dishonest, vain, gossiping creatures, whereas young men are more naive. Women were trained for life roles to some extent with dolls. Men are brought up playing with guns and playing Rugby, surely a preparation for possible war, that is, be familiar with guns and ready to respond to orders quickly during trench warfare and charge valiantly to likely death as so many men did at the Battle of Verdun for example, where some 2 million cannon shells were fired in a relatively short time.

Bottom line

Women catch their man-slaves by tarting themselves up, keeping their mouths shut about their sexual past and their real preferences (most women prefer the company of other women), and by using every deceitful artifice known to man to con you.

The result is an orchestrated symphony with several instruments, including:

- Lies
- Tears.
- Seduction.
- Enticement.
- Persuasion.
- Pleas.
- Asking.
- Begging.
- Bullying.
- Temper tantrums.

When a man is caught by such means by a wily woman he becomes a prisoner of the War of the Sexes, a man-slave, effectively a eunuch to provide for the woman's needs which include gratification, status, money, sex, children, and power over the husband and children. Thus she becomes boss and the husband the cannon fodder. Once he has sowed his seed(s) in her, he is expendable.

Young men would do well to be warned, therefore, that the biological purpose of a female is to breed and women are in part controlled by the devastating maternal instinct which is further discussed in Chapter 6.

Young boys on the other hand, are more interested in trying out sex with girls, as they must almost inevitably do at some point in life. They have not been brought up playing with dolls and so forth and are completely unprepared for the massive change in life that having children brings, whereas most girls are virtually preconditioned for it, almost salivating at the sight of babies and even pets.

Fortunately, however, the male contraceptive pill has almost arrived and one hopes that it is highly effective and reliable, and also cheap, but I fear the latter outcome is highly unlikely.

I would urge governments, therefore, to subsidize it as much as possible when it does appear because, of course, the world's human population is far too great already and, indeed, threatens our long term survival (Mohr, 2012c).

Chapter 3

MEN AND WOMEN
ARE VERY DIFFERENT

*Let's begin with a case study.
Our subject is feminist heroine Eve Ensler,
the author-impresario behind the worldwide
theatrical phenomenon 'The Vagina Monologues.
This was followed by 'The Good Body', a one-woman
show centering on Ensler's tormented relationship
with her slightly protruding post-forties abdomen.*
Laura Kipnis,
The Female Thing, Dirt, Sex, Envy, Vulnerability (2007).

History

That circa 99% of our DNA is shared with chimps indicates, of course, that we are animals, albeit having developed an enlarged cerebral cortex to store the semantic memory needed for our advanced language.

With the evolution of Homo sapiens, however, we became hunter-gatherers, whether as Neanderthal troglodytes or in grass huts on African plains. The women, obliged to care for their frequent offspring, had to leave the task of hunting to the men, though in some primitive African tribes today the women still do most of the gathering.

As with many other species, it was the males who had the task of defending their group. This led to men becoming bigger than, and having more muscle than women.

Another factor in this, perhaps, was the competitive alpha male scenario also seen in a few other species, particularly baboons that extend male hierarchy through the whole group (Weiss & Mann, 1978).

Physical differences

About one anatomical difference Kipnis (2007) writes:

Recall that Freud's slightly contentious phrase for this bedrock female sense of inadequacy was "penis envy" – which just sounds so retro these days. Who wants some fleshy old appendage swinging between her legs? **Not us**, *we're quite happy with our own equipment, thank you!*

As always from feminists, their discussion never gets much beyond sex. It never gets cerebral, not for long at least, as women don't, indeed can't have Newtonian powers of concentration upon problems of any real gravity, as discussed further in Chapter Five.

Other physical differences are that, as noted in the previous section, males are usually larger and have more muscle.

Women, on the other hand have more adipose tissue, some of it stored in the breasts for the mothering function. This greater amount of fat storage also allows the average woman to survive about four months without food, whereas the average male can only survive about a month before his body begins to shut down, blindness being one of the first results.

To allow greater physical activity men have coarser skin with more sweat glands to assist use of their larger muscle mass.

A larger, more muscled hunter, of course, is not as calming a sight as a smaller, weaker, and 'softer' woman so that, when they are in their prime, at least, women tend to be more attractive.

Indeed, in modern society they go to a great deal of trouble and expense to look nice. Sometimes, however, this is with farcical results, a primitive example being the enormous plates women of some Ethiopian tribes put in their lower lip to attract a husband. A comparable modern example, perhaps, are high heeled shoes.

Chemical differences

There are, of course many metabolic differences between men and women. For example, to help cope with their larger amounts of adipose tissue women have higher HDL levels to assist in reverse cholesterol transport. For similar reasons they can also tolerate higher homocysteine levels without ill-effects.

Hormones are, of course a major difference, for example men having higher testosterone levels and women higher levels of oestrogens, the female sex hormones. Levels of sex hormones peak in the late teens, of course, and then slowly decline.

Then, of course, young men not being halfway wise and running on high testosterone levels in their still formative teens and twenties, they don't fully understand how easy it is for just one of thousands of sperm to find its mark after just one act of sexual intercourse – a vague term – I really mean act of breeding. The girl does understand all too well, on the other hand, for she has grown up playing with dolls and has a very good idea indeed how babies are produced.

She too is running on hormones somewhat, albeit different ones, for example oestrogen and progesterone.

Modern human females are much more highly oestrogenized than their recent ancestors.

An Oxford zoologist calculated that over a mere 200 years the average number of menstrual cycles experienced by a European woman in her lifetime had increased from about thirty to 450. Her calculation is based upon the menarche's occurring earlier and upon the infrequent pregnancies that modern women can expect to carry to term together with shorter periods of lactation.

If we add to this the artificially 'oestrogenized' condition of modern women post-menopause we end up with up to astonishing 600 or so cycles (Greer, 1999).

Little wonder that some women call menstruation "the curse" and that Caro and Fox (2008) consider that both 'the pill' and the tampon were very liberating for women.

The maternal instinct

Somewhat tongue in cheek, I regard the maternal instinct as a devastating thing and joke that I thank God each day that I don't have it. Women have it, just as I suppose many animal species do, in order to ensure that they care for and raise their offspring. In other words, in nature most of the growth and behaviour we see in plants and animals is written in their DNA and thus preprogrammed.

Thus for females of any species their raison d'etre is largely to reproduce, something young men would do well to understand rather than regard sex as something of a 'fun thing.' In fact, it is really a deadly serious matter. That we make such a big deal of a basic animal function, in fact, is one of the many clear signs of how incredibly stupid human beings are, another, of course, being our never-ending history of conflict and war.

The maternal instinct is discussed in more detail in Chapter Six.

Sociological differences

In all human societies we have traditionally developed different roles and behaviours for men and women.

Men, being bigger and stronger, and not tied down with children, have usually been the hunters and the warriors, comparable roles, of course, in that they both involve killing.

We perpetuate that by still training young boys to play sports like rugby, comparable to the 'do as you're told' (regardless) and 'charge' (the enemy). If men are somewhat more inclined to physical violence than women, therefore, it is hardly surprising.

Women, on the other hand, have always had to have the main, if not total, responsibility of raising and caring for children.

Thus women are more inclined to long gossip sessions in which they bare their souls, air their grievances, and backstab people they don't like, not entirely an admirable practice.

In almost all human societies there have been major differences in how men and women dress and behave.

Men, of course, will dress less brightly, and in other respects too in a manner more appropriate for hunting and fighting. Thus, indeed, the stupid modern man's business suit is, of course, related to typical army uniforms of the last couple of centuries. Not only that, men's stupid ties derive from the scarves Roman soldiers used to carry ready to bind sword wounds if need be.

Women, on the other hand, did not wear pants to the extent that they do now, perhaps for practical reasons in part relating to the problems of embarrassing menopausal flows before the invention of such things as the tampon.

And, of course, in modern Western society girls like to wear bright colours, for example pink for young girls, and bright blues and reds and so forth when they are older.

Girls, of course, are supposed to be 'nice,' so that not only must they dress accordingly, but they are supposed to behave accordingly as well.

An example might be the now old-fashioned but graceful and lady-like curtsy, in contrast to the usually stiff and stern handshake between potential enemies and combatants which is so appropriately used even in the boxing ring.

No better example of male stupidity is the Maori haka, once an overture to battle, and thus still used prior to international Rugby matches by New Zealand rugby teams. Such silly practices should be disallowed but, of course, as I often lament, in our overpopulated, decadent, and decaying societies we are, of course, well into *reverse evolution*.

Thus in our growing megacities violence and crime is steadily on the increase, vandalism is rife with sidewalks often littered with broken booze bottles, and graffiti covers a great many wall, fences, and train carriages.

In addition, the booze, gambling and sex industries continue to grow, all involving activities that can only be described as immoral and stupid.

Nevertheless, such industries encourage and play upon the sociological differences between men and women, for example young men being encouraged to drink beer for life:

The chief customers of the public house today are the elderly and middle-aged men. Unless you can attract the younger generation to take the place of the older men, there is no doubt that we shall have to face a steadily falling consumption ..... if we begin advertising in the press we shall see that the continuance of our advertising is contingent upon the fact that we get educational support as well in the same papers. In that way it is wonderful how you can educate public opinion, generally, without making it too obvious that there is a public campaign behind it all ...
Sir Edgar Saunders, Director of the Brewers' Society, Birmingham, 1930 (Sargent, 1979).

Women, on the other hand, are encouraged to drink wine as part of their gender stereotyping, Chardonnay having been particularly fashionable for the last decade or two.

Young women, on the other hand now often drink various Vodka concoctions, some of them appropriately pink, for example, and others called 'Vodka smoothies.'

Correspondingly, young men will drink Jim Beam and cola and the like, the very names obviously targeting males.

Gambling, particularly on horse racing, was usually done by men, of course, but now women like to tart themselves up for the special big racing events such as the Melbourne Cup or the Royal Oaks.

Now, however, by my count slightly more women than men are to be found perched in front of poker machines in pubs and clubs, an activity requiring comparable intelligence to that required by Skinner Boxes used for operant conditioning experiments on lab rats. This, indeed, is yet another example of our *reverse evolution.*

Another, of course, is the increase in homosexuality in modern societies. This involves, of course, a change in role play for one member of each participating couple, one being the 'doer' and one the victim.

Transvestites, however, remain relatively rare, though sex-change operations are now a good deal easier to get and more common than hitherto.

Women becoming more 'butch,' however, is widespread and, of course, comes part and parcel with Feb Lib.

Once, for example, jeans were, of course, intended for male labourers, but thanks to the ubiquitous marketing of the modern age a high proportion of women wear them day in, day out.

In the movies, where sixty years ago much more than a hint of sex was not allowed, now one increasingly sees women 'mounting' the man in sexual intercourse. Indeed, a previous edition of this book had 'Women Are Getting On Top' as a subtitle (Mohr, 2012

Tonight, indeed, I see that a new TV series called 'House Husbands' is about to premiere, another sign of the times and that men are slowly losing the 'War of the Sexes.'

Intelligence

As part of the usual Feb Lib bullshit, of course, is the claim that women are just as intelligent as men, if not more so. In fact, the Gaussian or Normal Distribution of human intelligence is slightly wider for men than for women, a point discussed in more detail in Chapter Five.

The result is that there are more males with exceptionally high IQ, perhaps explaining in part the fact that nearly all important pioneering efforts and scientific discoveries have been made by men, albeit exceptional ones usually.

Thanks to the different roles that have long existed in society, women are generally more capable at many things, for example looking after children, cooking, sowing and knitting, and so forth. Some of these things they are taught from an early age, however, for example playing with dolls and toy houses being an obvious preparation for these roles in later life.

If women are brought up able to cook and thus feed children that is a good thing. That they are more inclined to care about cleanliness is another in relation to protecting their children from bacterial infections.

In that context it still surprises me that male chefs are still presumed to be best, as evidenced in the many absurd cooking shows now on TV. In reality, however, hotel and restaurant kitchens have in the past usually been utterly filthy places, as described more than once in Orwell's first published book *Down and Out In London and Paris* (1933). For that reason, at least, I might feel happier if the chefs were women but, fortunately, health regulations and inspections are far stricter these days.

We continue to see male 'nerds' dominate the computer industry, and also the engineering profession, both requiring, of course, considerable numeracy.

Indeed, I recall the last (male as usual) President of Harvard University being widely chastised for remarking that he thought there were some differences in ability between men and women. Perhaps as a result, the current 'Prez' is a woman!

Sexual differences

Just about every adult knows where the 'hot spot' is for achieving male orgasm.

A German doctor Ernst Grafenberg discovered the *G-spot* in 1950. This is in the wall of the vagina halfway between its opening and the cervix or "where the clitoris should have been located" according to Kipnis (2007).

Myself, I like to say that sex (the act of) was God's joke on mankind and that one has to be very stupid not to see it.

In other words, to consider the act of breeding as a big deal, or indeed as an 'act of love', is clearly foolish, if not downright absurdly animalistic.

The body's largest organ is the epidermis and I, for one, would prefer right now to be in some tropical paradise on a nice sunny day receiving a nice gentle back massage from a good-looking and appropriately dressed woman. That I might enjoy looking at a well-built woman in a bikini is in part a result of the way we brainwash ourselves with images of beautiful women, in part suggestive always of the supposed joys of sex.

Indeed, the pleasure of nicer looking things, whether that be art, scenery, or symmetrical mathematical equations of any kind, is in the eye of the beholder, as the cliché goes.

The act of breeding, on the other hand, is really a somewhat dirty business. One friend of mine from schooldays, having had a few drinks admittedly, recently said that "women are nasty smelly things. That's why they have to wear perfume."

If that be true, the act of sex is in part responsible and I, for one, would not enjoy some fool 'getting his rocks off' and dumping his load of soon to be smelly semen into my body.

According to Kipnis (2007):

But dirt is a central category [of difference between the sexes] *for all humans because the whole concept of "dirtiness" is tied to smells and textures whose existence we generally prefer to deny – those shame-ridden bodily functions and messy body products that we civilized beings prefer to distance ourselves from. Obviously what dirt most resembles is . . .* **shit***. In other words, our own bodies are the culprits when it comes to dirt. The body is "a kind of animated, mobile dirt factory, excluding filth at every aperture," Dr Kubie informs us.*

Reverse evolution

As said more than once already, I see the human race as being well into *reverse evolution*. One result that has been observed, in part an unavoidable result of our greatly excessive population, is that our intelligence is decreasing (Vernon, 1960).

Another is that of male baldness, a sad and silly looking condition that can only be, surely, an evolutionary error of sorts for I cannot for the life of me think of any sound reason in the spirit of Charles Darwin's 'survival of the fittest' concept of evolution that would explain the increasingly prevalent phenomenon of male pattern baldness.

Other changes taking place are far higher incidence of breast cancer in women, greater prevalence of genital abnormalities in males at birth, and much lower testosterone levels and sperm counts in men (Mohr, 2012a; Mohr & Fear, 2016; Mohr et al., 2018a). These changes may be attributed to increasing levels of pollution but, nevertheless, that is an environmental factor and, therefore, still part of the evolutionary process.

So perhaps the bottom line is that, whatever they may be, men and women should 'settle their differences', that is, accept them for what they are, learn to live with them and, indeed, take advantage of them wherever possible.

That we have different sexual organs is one difference that I see no great advantage off now that the human population is at least twice, perhaps four times, that which is sustainable with any degree of comfort, if comfort means everybody having a TV, a PC, a car and so forth.

Indeed, I see a case for a substantial proportion of men and women having vasectomies or their 'tubes tied'. If they really think the act of breeding etcetera so important, then that way they might be able to waste more time doing it without unwanted results.

In that respect at least, the now old-fashioned Christian discouragement of sex before marriage made good sense. Myself I would be inclined towards less encouragement off 'habitual' sex after marriage. After all, rotting in bed till death with the same person is really insane and rather dreadful.

Chapter 4

MYTHS ABOUT MEN & WOMEN

*Beauty stands In the admiration only of weak minds
led captive.* John Milton, *Paradise Regained,* book 2, 1. 120.

*The reason there are so few female comics
is that few women can bear being laughed at.*
Anna Russell, *Sunday Times,* London (Aug. 23, 1957).

Beauty

Men are generally not the prettiest of sights. Reasons for this are in part evolutionary, of course, so they are bigger, have more muscle, perhaps showing some signs of a beard, and are perhaps in some stage of male pattern baldness. At best the more handsome men are at least bearable to look at to my eye.

Women in their prime, perhaps in the age range 20 to 30, however, are often quite attractive and, indeed, many go to great pains and expense to make sure that they are.

So it is that modern Western culture celebrates the shape of a well-built woman, that is, with at least somewhat prominent breasts, the wider hips that led to the term 'broads' in the USA in the middle of the last century, and long flowing hair.

With no beard their face looks much 'cleaner' and, usually with considerable help from facial creams and cosmetics, their facial skin is often relatively flawless.

Then, of course, their carefully plucked, shaped and tinted eyebrows look neat and attractive. Add to this a bit of not-too-obvious eye shadow and the look is, of course, quite attention grabbing.

Here, however, a word of caution. This is that women who overdo their makeup and use tons of it do so at their peril. If, for example, they have too much bright red lipstick that will, of course, tend to make them look like clowns.

Below the neck there is the bra to uplift and accentuate the 'boobs', an important beauty aid because as a woman gets older her tits droop, often alarmingly to the point of becoming almost flat, as one sees in photos of African women who have never worn a bra.

"Certainly women find pleasure and excitement in exposing their breasts to advantage, otherwise the Wonderbra would never have earned a nickel. Throughout human history breasts have been pushed about, lengthened, pulled and tied down, scarified, pushed up, pushed apart, shaped into shelves and balconies without apparent cleavage, and pushed together to exaggerate cleavage" (Greer, 1999).

Less used these days, the corset was once very widely used to pull in women's tummies and thus give them a more 'curvy' look. Then, of course, there are the flimsy panties, these days often absurdly 'thongs' in the form of a G-string to excite males when the woman gets undressed for sex.

Now for the outer layer of clothes.

To really attract attention a dress or top with a large vee at the front to show off cleavage will, of course, give the world a titillating indication of how good the boobies are. The skirt should then fit well around the waist to pull it in a little, further improving the overall figure.

Alternatively, of course, skin-tight pants, often black, will show off the hopefully cute bottom and legs well. To further accentuate the legs high heels will ensure an 'out there' style of walking akin to that seen so much on fashion catwalks.

Finally, add some powerful and expensive perfume to make the overall package smell nice and there you have it, the femme fatale.

Just to complete the picture, such a picturesque woman might have her man following a step or two behind dressed like a bum in expensive but cheap-looking jeans and shoes, with designer stubble to complement an already balding scalp, and a silly Tee shirt with some mindless lettering on it.

Sugar and spice and everything nice

We all know the rhyme containing that line and continuing with such bullshit as 'puppy dogs tails' for boys. It does say a lot about how we treat and bring up boys and girls somewhat differently, however, that is, girls are supposed to be nice whilst boys are supposed to be otherwise.

Sure girls are brought up trying to look nice and, to some extent at least, to behave nicely. On the behaviour front, of course, women's niceness is largely a front which all too often conceals a dark soul: a mean, selfish, bossy bitch.

Indeed, given the family life which she so often craves, that is, children, pets, constant support from all and sundry because she is a mother, 'mum' often becomes a little Hitler and bosses children around mercilessly (just watch this going on sometimes in supermarkets and the street) and puts the husband below the dog in the order of importance.

His job was always to work as a slave to 'bring home the bacon' and also to 'service' the woman with a little bedtime lubrication sometimes. Indeed, I once had a woman friend who was somewhat sympathetic towards the male problem of having to 'get it up' on cue, so to speak, regardless of the circumstances which might include tiredness, stress, distraction, low libido, being somewhat inebriated, and the woman being unattractive, if not somewhat ugly in reality.

Men are the sex fiends

It is generally assumed that men are the sex fiends in society and that women are totally virtuous.

Reporting on the celebrated research of Kinsey et al. (1953), Lindzey et al. (1978) say:

"- women are not as interested in the male body or the genitals as men are in the female body. Women prefer to have various parts of the body stimulated before being touched in the genitals. Kinsey's data did not indicate, however, whether these differences were a product of cultural conditioning or of other factors.

When the Kinsey reports first appeared, they seemed to confirm the general belief that men are oriented more toward sex or have a stronger sex drive than women. In recent years, quite a few writers have challenged the notion that this is an inborn difference. Many people now believe that women are just as sexually oriented as men, but that parental and social prohibitions have repressed their sexual expression. Leaders of the women's liberation movement are strongly urging women to free themselves from the sexual bondage to which society has committed them.

To confirm the latter sentences it is perhaps best if I give some comparatively modern quotations:

Woman has sex organs just about everywhere. She experiences pleasure almost everywhere. Luce Irigaray, 1986.

When I was fourteen, it was considered the hallmark of feminine success and popularity to be able to perform the perfect blow job. Naomi Wolf, 1997.

This is my favourite vibrator, the Pocket Rocket. Use it when you're in a traffic jam. Ava Cadell, sexologist.

It should also be noted that the extent of one's sexual desires may be circumstance dependent and the following situations are examples of this:

[1] In females oestrogen levels fluctuate a good deal during the menstrual cycle and in cats, for example,

*- there is a strong connection between the presence of large amounts of **estrogen**, the female hormone, in the blood and sexual behaviour. When lower animals are 'in heat,' the estrogen levels are high* (Morgan et al., 1979).

[2] *The pin-up girls in soldiers' barracks symbolize a fantasy life that goes on when normal social life with women is frustrated. Experiments have shown that men on a starvation diet lose their interest in women and instead hang on their walls pictures of prepared food cut from magazines* (Hilgard et. al, 1975).

[3] *Rats that are raised in isolation mate normally the first time they are tested. But with monkeys, chimpanzees, and humans, the story is quite different. Monkeys that are raised in isolation must learn to mate, and they may be so socially impaired by early isolation that they have great difficulty with this learning* (Harlow, 1962). *And the well-known variations — including the so-called aberrations — of human sexual behaviour make it obvious that learning and experience play a tremendously important role in our expression of the sexual drive* (Morgan et al., 1979).

In conclusion it can be safely said that sex drive is circumstance dependent, for example if you are down and out and living on the street you might think most about cold and hunger and very little about sex, if at all.

It can also be said that female sex drive, though perhaps more concealed because of societal constraints, is at least in the 'same ballpark' as that of men. Indeed, somewhere about the middle of the menstrual cycle female sex drive may peak at higher levels than those of most men.

As for men 'perving' over voluptuous women in men's magazines, women too perv over men, sometimes also unclothed, in women's magazines. Indeed, as a young child I recall staying with a very religious aunt once: she had me and her husband shower together in an old-fashioned shower in the bathtub and perved over this sight.

Similarly, I once heard the wife of my eldest brother going into raptures perving about a particularly big and strong football player whose team her husband followed.

Nowadays, as Lewis (2005) notes:

In the wake of the Chippendales, hundreds of copycat troupes sprung up, such that male stripping is now a part of life. Following the success of the British film 'The Full Monty', in which a bunch of average-looking unemployed blokes and cash-strapped tradesmen turn themselves into strippers to turn an honest coin, we now cannot move for ordinary men taking off their clothes.

Related to this is the growing male escort business that is, in effect, prostitution. A sign of things to come in this area, a woman experienced in the brothel business, Heidi Fleiss, is planning to open a "stud farm" or brothel for women clients in the desert town of Crystal in Nevada.

As for the sex industry, traditionally and still involving mostly women, that is some evidence that women are not only capable of far higher levels of sexual activity than men, but also compelling evidence that women are far more unscrupulous than men are not so much influenced by 'nice' emotions such as love as is supposed.

The weaker sex?

Women have long been called the weaker sex, and, indeed, they are usually smaller and have a good deal less muscle and a good deal more adipose tissue.

Indeed, the breasts usually contain a good deal of the latter for men to perv over. In contrast, however, women often perv over muscular men.

Thus women are, on average, physically weaker, but whether they are intellectually or emotionally weaker is another matter. The intelligence issue is referred to briefly later in this chapter, and at greater length in Chapter Five.

As for emotional strength, there is no doubt that women are more easily reduced to tears. Indeed, that Freud and Jung based so many psychiatric conditions upon their mostly women patients annoys many women.

When angry, women can turn on incredible tantrums that can endure all too long for comfort.

When angry men are more inclined to violence, no doubt in part a cultural issue as they are brought up playing rough sports like rugby which often involve 'punch ups.'

Women, however, are very capable of violence, we just hear less about it because men are less likely to complain about it. Indeed, I myself have been witness to and victim of spectacular displays of physical violence by women on occasion, and I mention an example in Chapter Two.

On another occasion spending an evening at a woman friend's house I was playing a tape of King's College Choir. She piped up with: "Turn that rubbish off" or some such.

I replied: "You'd f--- donkeys wouldn't you."

That was it. She started hitting me about the face and could not stop. I had to catch a taxi home circa midnight on a Saturday, not easy to do when your face is covered in blood!

It must be admitted that my perfunctory utterance was exactly of the sort that pro football players sometimes use to 'suck in' opponents to hitting them in the hope that they will be 'rubbed out' by the referees.

All too often women get emotional to the extent of 'verbal assault' and thus induce physical assault from their partner. After, say, ten years of marriage with the stresses of children, job stresses, job and money insecurity, and simply lack of privacy and 'space,' at least an occasional argument is inevitable but as much effort as possible should then be made at reconciliation afterwards for, of course, marriage break-ups are now epidemic and doing great harm to our society and the next generation of it.

Women are honest or 'genuine'

Women, often looking nicer, of course tend to appear more honest and thus be more persuasive.

In fact, however, throughout history women have tended to be far better and more prolific liars than men. Being supposedly 'nice' and all that bullshit, of course, some of them think they can do no wrong and will be exceedingly affronted if any suggestion to the contrary is made.

For example, women like to indulge in gossip, particularly with other women, often in group sessions. Most gossip is about other people, of course, indeed women's magazines are full of it about movie stars, for example.

Indeed, many somewhat psycho women will 'spill the dirt' on anybody they can, including their immediate family, at every opportunity. In my own case a backstabbing wife was the "Judas' that instigated the end of my promising University career, an act for which she has no regret.

Indeed, it is no exaggeration to say that, during my disastrous marriage to this psychopathic bully, I could not waggle my knee a little, a common habit for many people, without being called mad behind my back.

The bottom line, really, is that women are the ultimate liars.

Just one example often occurs in courtship, that is, the women will want to know as much as she can about a man's 'love life' past and present, whereas she will tend to deny any sort of past sex life, or at least dismiss is as inconsequential.

Traditionally, of course, we make use of the natural lying ability of women by using them as office receptionists so that they can say, for example, that their boss is "busy" when, in fact, he might be playing golf or having a booze session.

Women also tend to be at least somewhat self-righteous. Indeed, some will admit to no wrongs or faults at all and certainly when marriages break up, the husband is usually blamed for just about everything that went wrong.

Women have different abilities

The penultimate president of Harvard University (a male as usual) was almost pilloried after saying that he thought that men had somewhat different abilities from women. Feb Lib had their revenge: the current 'Prez' is a woman.

Traditionally, of course, women have had the task of raising children and housekeeping, a situation that has changed a great deal in recent decades as rampant capitalism gradually reduces the real standard of living for working people, spouting dishonest and incompetent econobabble as an excuse for this injustice.

But there must be innate differences. In some parts of Africa, at least, average IQ is only circa 70. In contrast, it has been proved that Negroes have DNA differences that make them better sprinters.

Men and women have different DNA and, therefore, must have some differences in competencies. Having more muscle men are slightly better athletes, whereas the smaller more nimble fingers of women may have always been better suited to such activities as sowing and are now preferred by some industries such as assembly lines for electronic products.

History would also suggest that men are better and deeper thinkers, and more prolific inventors, though now with more women than men attending University in some countries, that situation might change, but I do not think it will change dramatically, in part because most women still want to have children, a major distraction, of course.

There is no doubt, however, that men on average have better mathematical skills (Vernon, 1960; Morgan et al, 1975).

Indeed, the Gaussian distribution of IQ spreads wider for men, a point discussed further in the following Chapter.

Women are better communicators

It is sometimes claimed that women are better communicators, no doubt in part because of the 'mother's club' that began with as often as not pregnant women sitting around in groups with their children while their husbands went hunting and gathering.

I would contend, however, that what counts is the quality of the communication, not the quantity.

Indeed, my fifth grade teacher, Miss Bachelard, often implored we students to produce quality, not quantity.

Thus I would not count the 'waffle' that women produce in their frequent gossip sessions as being of much value.

Instead, comparable to the way in which I define 'real IQ' in the next Chapter, I would prefer to have 'useful', constructive, and informative communication that leads to some real, positive outcome as a result of increasing my knowledge and understanding of some issue or problem that may interest or concern me.

Thus it is that I deplore the endless tripe that pours out night and day from the media. Rarely does it really get to the bottom of most issues and thus put itself in a position, at least, to tell the truth without bias or constraints. Instead, most of the output is just a form of gossip, as indeed are the all too frequent panel shows where the panel might as well just talk to each other and turn of the cameras and not waste our time with yet more drivel.

Very rarely are any hard numbers given to explain the magnitude of a problem, the only exception being:

(a) The weather forecasts put at the end of the news so you have to watch all the ads and other BS first.

(b) The stock market indices which, of course, fluctuate rather like the weather in the short term at least.

The gossip amongst women has much in common with the media news, that is, they update each other on the goings-on amongst their family and acquaintances.

Men, on the other hand, are more likely to talk about how the football team they fancy is faring, for example. In other words in the workplace or pub they too talk a load of crap.

The bottom line is that I think that on the communication issue, regardless of quantity, men and women both talk crap by and large, and only rarely does anyone say anything particularly new, intelligent, and which improves the sorry lot of mankind even one iota.

Conclusion

There are, of course, many myths about women and our decadent Western societies place them on a pedestal and proclaim their great beauty and virtue whilst Feb Lib continues to argue for their advancement. At present, indeed, women are edging ahead, it seems.

The few issues discussed in preceding sections seek to dispel some of these myths whilst the major issue of differences in intelligence is discussed at modest length in the following Chapter.

Morgan et al. (1979) conclude on differences between men and women:

[1] "Girls excel in verbal ability." "Group differences average about 4 points on a verbal IQ measure."

[2] "Boys excel in visual-spatial ability. This superiority appears consistently in adolescence and adulthood, not earlier, and reaches an average level of about 6 points on an IQ-like measure."

[3] "Boys excel in mathematical ability." "It averages somewhat less than the difference in spatial ability and may be related to it."

[4] "Males are more aggressive. This sex difference has been observed in many lower species as well as most, if not all, human cultures. It can be observed very early, as soon as social play begins. Most male aggression is directed toward other males."

In the latter regard, the deplorable alpha male phenomenon that some men also seem to possess is worth note as it plays a major role in the lives of some animal species.

Noted 'Marxist feminist' Evelyn Reed entitled an article:

Is Man an "Aggressive Ape"

with perhaps some historical justification, also deploring the widespread use by historians of the term "mankind" because is it "left womankind entirely out of the picture."

She also said:

A currently fashionable school of writers claims that the study of animals proves that humans are innately aggressive, and that war is a biological necessity. This pseudoscientific theory attempts to legitimize war, and disorients opponents of war (Reed, 1970).

These days, with women beginning to win the War of the Sexes, however, I am happy to remind the reader that gray wolves have an 'alpha pair' that are the only ones in the pack that breed. Thanks to Fem Lib I think it could be said that there are human alpha females also.

In that context, a word of caution to naïve young men intrigued by nicely dressed women with almost perfect makeup. Brigadier General Custer might have said, had he survived the battle of Little Bighorn, do not trust people with painted faces.

Chapter 5

THE GAUSSIAN DISTRIBUTION OF IQ

*There are, it should be noted, considerable sex differences,
females being relatively superior in spelling
and inferior in arithmetic [results for 15-year olds].
Many surveys of intelligence and attainments have also
demonstrated that the range or spread of ability
(as distinct from the average performance)
is slightly more restricted in girls.*
P.E. Vernon, *Intelligence and Attainment Tests,*
University of London Press (1960).

History

As we evolved as hunter-gatherers, and thus with men and women having somewhat different roles, it follows that men and women must have developed and passed on through the generations somewhat different skill levels for various activities.

For example, the men being the hunters were stronger and developed the greater aggression needed for hunting.

Women, on the other hand, were largely responsible for child rearing, pretty much a full-time job when little was known about preventing conception. Thus women had many children but because child mortality rates were high relatively few of them survived to adulthood. Raising children, of course, involves a very different skill set indeed from that of hunting.

With the Agricultural Revolution new and increasingly diverse occupations emerged and men, of course, took up these and all but a few women were still left with the task of caring for a family.

It was thus men who developed philosophy, arts, science and technology and built towns and cities, all too often fighting wars to defend them against advancing armies directed by power-hungry rulers.

Less than three hundred years ago the Industrial Revolution began, bringing with it machines and factories that greatly changed lifestyles. Again, all the inventions that came with the Industrial Revolution were made by men.

Advanced education was then required to train people for new occupations in society such as law, medicine and engineering. Almost invariably this was for men, of course, though, no doubt because of their traditional caring role with families, it was always women that were apprenticed as nurses and midwives.

So it was that, only about a hundred years ago, Cambridge University only had male academic staff and students.

Some part of all this evolutionary history must have been passed on in the differing DNA for men and women. In addition, just as epigenic marking passes on traits such as obesity, so to it must be able to pass on traits such as higher level thinking and the like.

Ability differences

As noted in the previous chapter:

[1] Women tend to have greater verbal ability, no doubt developed in their traditional child rearing role for, quite simply, it was they who had to teach children language.

[2] Men have greater visual-spatial ability, doubtless developed in their role as hunter-gatherers.

[3] Men have greater mathematical ability, no doubt because it was they who developed mathematics and science and then worked in the technological occupations that developed from scientific advances. To give a trivial example, not much arithmetic is involved, if any, in teaching a child to count. On the other hand, at least some skill in arithmetic is involved in building, for example measuring the number, sizes, and spans of rafters required to build a roof.

[4] Men are stronger and more aggressive, having had to be so as hunters, but not much more intelligence is required for this activity compared to child rearing.

Nerds

Given their lesser ability at maths I should not be surprised if most women were confused by the occasional equation in this book. As Stephen Hawking said about his book *A Brief History of Time* (Hawking, 1989):

Each equation . . . . in the book would halve the sales.

Hawking occupies the Professorship at Cambridge University once occupied by Newton. Today Newton would have been described as a nerd, a negative term now applied to smart young men. Typical of many very high IQ people he was a loner, having come from a peasant background to study at Cambridge perhaps being an isolating factor. He retired from Cambridge at 42 after 3 nervous breakdowns, in part perhaps because of a fire which destroyed 20 years of his work:

He lived the life of a solitary, and like all men who are
occupied with profound meditation, he acted strangely.
Sometimes in getting out of bed, an idea would come to him,
and he would sit on the edge of the bed,
half dressed, for hours at a time.
Louis Figuier, *Vies de Savants* (tr. B.H. Clark, 1897).

The Gaussian distribution

The Gaussian distribution is perhaps the cornerstone of modern statistics. It is a 'bell-shaped' curve that plots the probability of a randomly distributed variable deviating from a mean value by a certain amount.

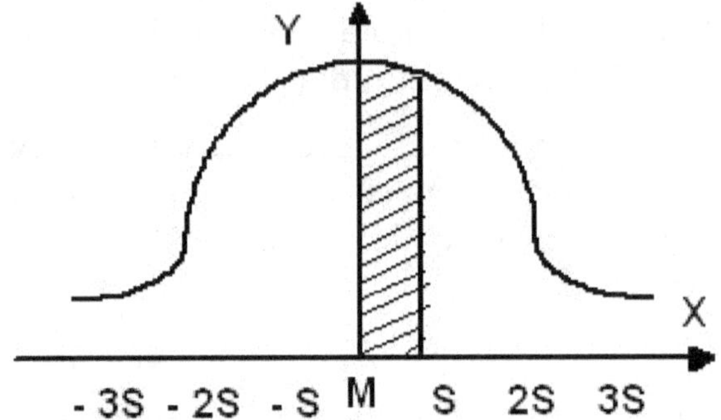

Figure 5.1. The Gaussian distribution.

It is usually called the Normal Distribution because we *normalize* the horizontal scale, scaling in terms of the *standard deviation* S (also shifting the origin to X = M, the mean or average value of all X values) as shown in Figure 5.1.

The *probability density function* is

$$Y = [1/\mathrm{sqr}(2\ \mathrm{pi}\ S^2] \exp[\ -\ (X - M)^2/2S^2]$$

with standard deviation S = sqr[Sum$(X - M)^2$/(N-1)]
where
N is the number of X values, sqr[ ] = square root
pi = ratio of a circle circumference to its diameter = 3.14159
and exp[ ] is the exponential function.

The constant 'pi' appears in the formula because its derivation involves calculating the square of the integral of the exponential term using polar coordinates in order to ensure that the total area under the curve in Figure 5.1 (i.e., the total possible probability) equals 1.

Tables for the normal distribution usually give the area hatched in Figure 5.1 that is

$$p(0 \leq X - M \leq kS) = 0.34 \text{ for } k=1$$

so that the probability p( ) of X deviating from the mean M by the amount M is 0.34 or 34%, and probability of deviation twice this amount, or k = 2, is approximately 48%.

As a simple everyday example, a machine part is made with a mean diameter of 1.535 cm and a standard deviation S of 0.005. The probability that a part has a diameter between 1.535 and 1.543 cm is given by calculating

$$z = (X - M)/S = (1.543 - 1.535)/0.005 = 1.6$$

for which the normal distribution probability is 44.5%.

It turns out, however, that the Gaussian distribution of intelligence, as measured by the Weschler scales, for example, is significantly wider for men than women, though it does have about the same mean.

That means more male geniuses or 'nerds', but also more males at the bottom of the IQ scale, and perhaps some of these, given no better choice, are amongst the criminals in our societies, though not likely to be the 'brains' behind anything but the most trivial and small-scale crimes.

This reality does a lot, perhaps, to explain human history, on the positive side helping explain why it was almost always men who did the long and deep thinking and made the important scientific discoveries.

Real IQ

Intelligence is part inherited and part developed thereafter by learning and experience, often referred to as 'nature and nurture.' It is sometimes argued that IQ tests only measure learning but, in fact, they are "a standardized examination devised to measure human intelligence as distinct from attainments" (Carter, 2007).

It is generally assumed that our IQ peaks at the age of 18, about when 'developmental' school education is finished in advanced countries. I contend that further education and study, however, should be able to increase IQ further so I propose a *real IQ* calculated for those over 18 as

$$\text{Real IQ} = \text{IQ}(18) - a(\text{disease/injuries})$$
$$+ \; b(\text{years of learning since 18})$$
$$+ \; c(\text{creativity}) - d[(\text{age} -18) \text{ if over 18}]$$

Here IQ(18) is that one develops, all going OK, by age 18 as a result of hereditary factors and education, and

(a) 'a' is a constant to calculate reduction in IQ resulting from any disease or injuries acquired later which affect the brain, including Alzheimer's disease and psychiatric conditions such as depression.[1]

(b) 'b' is a constant, perhaps circa 0.25, for the effect of learning after the age of 18.

(c) 'c' is a constant for creativity, perhaps circa 1 – 2 if creativity is measured on a scale of 1 to 10.

(d) 'd' is a constant for normal decline in intelligence with aging, perhaps about half the value of the constant 'b'.

In the terms involving the factors 'b' and 'd' the notion of 'use it or lose it' is considered, that is, learning doing intelligent things should help further increase one's intelligence, just as doing more exercise should help strengthen one's muscles.

Creativity is obviously an important factor because if one has considerable ability, but no inclination to put it to tangible use, then one cannot be seen as having much real intelligence. Whether creativity is, to any extent, in one's genes is debatable, but probably it is mostly a learnt trait, but one that nevertheless relates to intelligence. In other words, without much ability to create, or intelligence, one is not likely to be very creative.

---

[1] In contrast to depression, note that positive attitudes may improve real intelligence, an example being the 'teacher expectancy effect.'

The foregoing simple equation should, indeed, encourage people to indulge in vicarious learning, surely the best kind for usually people are able to tackle subjects that genuinely interest them with more enthusiasm. In addition, being free to choose when and how one studies may improve results, of course, as this is far less painful than the all too many years spent listening to morons at school and University regurgitate material from text books they have little understanding of, and have often only read themselves recently.

In my view, it also helps explain how people like Leonardo da Vinci and Isaac Newton, despite having only had very basic schooling, could achieve so much.

As for men vs. women, I would contend that, in addition to the wider Gaussian distribution of intelligence for men noted earlier, men have traditionally had to develop more knowledge and intelligence to pursue their work, particularly as advances in knowledge and technology made that more complex.

In addition, of course, in the traditionally mostly male workforce were the exceptionally clever 'nerds' that made all the clever discoveries and inventions, perhaps establishing something of a tradition in that regard also.

Reverse evolution

In *The Descent of Man* Charles Darwin cited the work of his cousin Francis Galton more than ten times. Galton did much important scientific work, including proposing and defining the term *eugenics*, on which subject Darwin wrote:

We civilized men, on the other hand, do our utmost to check the process of elimination; we build asylums for the imbecile, the maimed, and the sick; we institute poor-laws; and our medical men exert their utmost skill to save the life of every one to the last moment. Thus the weak members of civilized societies propagate their kind.

In addition, modern medical science is able to keep alive people with serious genetic disorders and there is concern in some quarters that this will lead to a deterioration of the human gene pool:

Many people are born each year with genetic defects that in the past would have hampered their reproductive potential. Now, medical treatment enables them to survive, reproduce, and pass on the defective genes. Followers of this view, such as the Nobel Prize winning geneticist H.J. Mueller, see this tampering with selection as a black cloud hanging over our future. Someday, Mueller says, all people will be born with one major genetic problem or another: diabetes, PKU, hemophilia.
M.L. Weiss, A.E. Mann,
Human Biology and Behaviour (1978).

The results? Vernon (1960) points out that a Royal Commission on Mental Deficiency in the UK discovered a "big increase" in the numbers of defectives between the years 1907 and 1929.

Carlo Cipolla (1974) pointed out that our population growth graph went almost vertical with the coming of the industrial revolution and implored that what we needed was 'quality not quantity,' a phrase I recall my fifth grade teacher Miss Bachelard repeating often.

Vernon (1960) and Lynn and Vanhaven (2002) point out that we have dysgenic fertility trends so that the least intelligent people have the most children. Burt (1957) found that average IQ in the UK had dropped by 1.5% between the years 1920 and 1950 for this reason and he predicted a further 2.5% drop by the year 2000.

It has also been suggested that IQ in the USA is in decline (Fancher, 1985), some claiming that the rate of decrease is 1 point per generation.

The picture is far worse from a global point of view. Average IQ in Africa is only 70 and, of course, it is in such places that population has exploded in the last century while population growth in more advanced countries has ground to a halt.

The bottom line, therefore, is that, on average, the human race has become a good deal dumber simply as a result of demographic reasons. Considering that even the most intelligent of us in modern consumer societies, however, have been also reduced to brainwashed idiots in part, at least, the overall situation is grim to say the least (Mohr, 2012a; Mohr & Fear, 2016; Mohr et al., 2018a).

The implications of declining average intelligence are far reaching. It has been shown that a drop of just 3 points in average IQ results in increasing numbers of:

(a) Men in jail - 13%.

(b) High school dropouts (permanent) - 15%.

(a) Women chronically dependent on welfare - 15%.

The bottom line, therefore, is that we are into reverse evolution both mentally and physically, in part because eugenics became a dirty word because of ill-conceived attempts at reducing 'bad breeding,' for example:

(a) From 1907, 27 US states passed sterilization laws to prevent such people as epileptics, the feeble-minded, habitual criminals, and 'moral perverts' from having children. In most states these laws were not enforced but in California 10,000 people were sterilized by 1935.

(b) Other countries including Denmark, Germany, Norway, Sweden and Switzerland passed similar laws, in Sweden 60,000 young women being sterilized between 1935 and 1976.

(c) Eugenics was supposedly the justification for the massive extermination programs of the scientists and geneticists of the Third Reich, leading to the stigma attached to the word.

In the economically decaying West, having spent the best part of a century fighting socialism, we have now have gone too far in our quest for equality, insisting that regardless of sex, race or any other factor, we are all equal. We have dumbed down our education systems, our political systems, and our 'consumer zombie' society in general in which we now breed 'willy-nilly,' perhaps with a quick copulatory act between yet another raft of mindless TV ads.

As our society regresses it is now, once again in history, more and more a fight for survival in an increasingly fierce economic rat race whilst the planet's resources and its environment gradually diminish in quantity and quality.

My father, despite having had 3 children (I was the third!), believed in ZPG (zero population growth), quite correctly at that time.

Since then China has had its one-child policy and has become the world's second largest and strongest economy.

Myself, told by a woman I had made pregnant that the child would be "mildly retarded", I consulted some experts who inferred that 'mildly' was really quite serious. I then persuaded the woman to have an abortion though 5 months pregnant. She did, about which I have no conscience.

David Galton concludes that: *Society as a whole should embrace the new* [eugenics] *technology and the opportunities it offers less timorously, or even with some measure of enthusiasm* (Galton, 2001).

Conclusions

With more and more women at University and in the workforce, differences in ability and intelligence between men and women are likely to be reduced. Indeed, in part owing to bad cultural influences, boys are tending to do worse than girls on average at school, in part because more of them drop out early.

Of greater concern is that, because of excessive and indiscriminate breeding, human intelligence is declining significantly. Indeed our excessive population, along with such factors as pollution, resource depletion and global warming, threatens our long term survival (Mohr, 2012c).

I would contend that modern humans living in air conditioned homes in megacities and only having to heat up supermarket foods are far less resourceful and 'practically intelligent' than hunter-gatherers had to be.

Sadly, the day of the lone researcher and inventor are fast disappearing with huge research teams now being the norm in medical and pharmaceutical research, for example.

This reduction in intelligence of our dangerously overgrown human population I refer to as *reverse evolution* (Mohr, 2012a; Mohr & Fear, 2016; Mohr et al., 2018a).

Chapter 6

THE MATERNAL INSTINCT

Teenagers are hormones with legs on and not much else.
What I would have done for a boy or man I loved when I was
fourteen, fifteen, sixteen – things I would most certainly
not do now. That is the problem for us.
Remaining single is not really a choice, it's a sentence.
The idea of life without a man,
without children, seems impossible.
Elizaberth Wurtzel, *Bitch*, 1998.

The maternal instinct

MRI scans of mothers' brains show that they do indeed have a maternal instinct. Is it passed on in the female genes in some animal species, or is it a learnt trait, or does this seemingly powerful instinct come, like intelligence, from both *nature* and *nurture*?

Maternal genes are required for the normal development of the embryo. These genes determine the basic body plan of the embryo before fertilization takes place. Does fertilization with an additional X chromosome somehow give rise, at least in part, to the maternal instinct?

I suspect that this must necessarily be the case in many animal species to ensure the survival of the species. With all life forms physical form and growth is largely preprogrammed by DNA.

6. The Maternal Instinct

All animal species, except humans it seems, are born knowing how to walk, for example. With humans, thanks to our relatively large brain size needed to store the semantic memory needed for our advanced languages, we are not born knowing many basic functions such as walking. Indeed, our brain size is limited at birth by the physical capacity of the vagina to allow passage of the foetus, and this is why many neural connections such as those needed for walking develop after birth, a great many neural connections being formed in the first two or three years of human life.

If we are 'short on neural wiring' then why would human females be 'preloaded' with a maternal instinct?

If males, on the other hand, are normally more aggressive at almost the first opportunity, such as in toddler playgroups, then why should not females be naturally more inclined for a caring role and thence have the maternal instinct in some degree as soon as they are old enough and given the opportunity to express it.

Then, of course, there are great exceptions, for example male Emperor Penguins care for their offspring while the females hunt for food. It would seem, however, that such a clear cut reversal of roles must be 'preprogrammed' in the DNA at birth.

I am therefore inclined to believe that, in humans, females are born with a 'basic' maternal instinct, but also that this is initially dormant but develops and strengthens as girls grow into women, so that ultimately having children becomes a raison d'etre. Then, when they have children the instinct to care for them becomes as dominant an instinct as that for their own survival.

It should also be emphasized that the maternal instinct has two key parts:

(1) The 'maternal wish' that makes women want to have children.

(2) A strong impulse to care for their children.

Social learning

Whether girls are born with a maternal instinct or not, it normally begins at an early age and is reinforced by social learning, particularly being given dolls and doll houses as toys, and perhaps imitating their mother's role of caring for both themselves and other children in the family.

Then, of course, once they reach puberty there is, as with boys, inevitably the question of trying out acts of sex, ultimately including sexual intercourse, sooner or later.

As they get older, of course, women will see some of their friends and relatives having children and will be bound to consider, and ultimately decide, to do likewise.

So whether or not the maternal instinct is innate, there is plenty of opportunity for it to develop from scratch and then strengthen considerably, becoming a powerful force when a woman has children.

Motherhood

There is no doubt that motherhood is a life-changing experience. In *The Whole Woman* Greer (1999) writes:

The experience of falling desperately in love with one's baby is by no means universal but it is an occupational hazard for any woman at birth. Most of the women who find themselves engulfed in the emotional tumult of motherhood are astonished by the intensity of the bliss that suddenly invades them and the keenness of the anguish they feel when their child is in pain or trouble.

On a more negative note Greer says:

Motherhood is regarded now as a sort of personal indulgence. Cracker-barrel psychologists tell us that mothers become mothers out of carelessness or selfishness or narcissism or because they want something to love.

Such remarks are a bit over the top, perhaps because Greer never had children. Indeed, from her earlier largely 'sex-envy' based writings right up to this day, her views are often somewhat ignorant and/or biased, to say the least. Indeed, from the outset she seems to have merely wanted to create a little controversy and bathe in the limelight that gave her.

Animal experiments

Seitz (1954), experimenting with 60 female albino rats, gave some of them litters of 3, 6, 9 or 12 baby rats. He found an almost linear inverse correlation between maternal behaviour and litter size.

The situation became more complex when mothers with initially small litter sizes were given large second litters, and vice versa. Maternal behaviour increased when the second litter was small, but did not decrease when it was large, presumably because stronger maternal behaviour had been learnt with the small first litter.

One conclusion I draw from this is that, particularly with the human population now far too great, it is wiser to have only a couple of children at most.

Another might be that staff to child ratios in day care centres need to be fairly high compared to those at schools, especially for very young children.

Conclusion

Whether or not human females are born with it to some 'primary' extent or not, the maternal instinct is certainly learnt and reinforced from early childhood, becoming a very powerful force when women have children.

Indeed, before then young women are likely to be strongly influenced by the importance and status that society places on the role of motherhood, and also by the apparent satisfaction and sense of achievement that motherhood brings to women.

In fact, of course, since our troglodyte days we humans have lived primarily in family groups, as do, of course, a great many animal species.

It is not natural or normal to live alone and breeding is, of course, necessary for the survival of every species. Thus women will usually follow the lead of their own parents and also want to have children, and thus find a man to have those children with.

I do not believe this is a matter of 'love,' a greatly overused and misused word which in concept is, at best, largely ethereal. I believe it is a matter of 'the way of things', of how normal human society has, like that of a great many animal species, operated.

Indeed, I believe the urge to have children is something of a raison d'etre for women. Moreover, having 'shacked up' with a man, without children life staring at just that one other face can quickly get a little boring as one slowly runs out of new things to talk about and do.

With growing and learning children about, on the other hand, there is always their progress to observe and their experiences to share. A steady state of flux, indeed, that keeps parents busy, if not excessively so in the case of larger families.

Now, however, because our population is already far too great to be sustainable, we should avoid unwanted pregnancies, plan only for a couple of children at most, and ensure that our marriages are stable and likely to last before having children. We owe that, at least, to our children.

Bottom line

Finally, I would like to urge young men to beware of the powerful maternal instinct. All too often, if not usually, young men, not having been brought up with dolls and so forth, are blissfully ignorant of just what pregnancy and having children entails.

Moreover, they have little or no understanding of the probability of just one sperm of perhaps a couple of million finding its way to its mark and producing a child nine months later.

In this regard, that the Christian and other religions forbad sex before marriage was a good, practical thing, for at least people had made the commitment of marriage before having children.

Nowadays big business and technology have largely displaced religion in the West, but at least it might be hoped that, with the advent of the male contraceptive pill, young men might be able to prevent unwanted pregnancies. Indeed, with teen mums on the increase and 50% divorce rates I hope that the male pill is as cheap as possible, perhaps with the help of government subsidies.

Indeed, as a practical measure I would hand them out at school, just as condoms were sometimes handed out when groups of soldiers went on leave.

Chapter 7

GIRLS & BOYS & THEIR TOYS

From them [girl's magazines] *the emerging girl learns
that the only life worth living is a life totally out of control,
disrupted by debt, disordered eating,
drunkenness, drugs, and casual sex.*
Germaine Greer, *The Whole Woman* (1999).

Introduction

That men and women are very different has already been
discussed at some length in earlier chapters, particularly
Chapters 3 and 5. A great many of those differences, of
course, arise from different upbringing in childhood and from
the conventions of the particular society in which they live.

In the early years imprinting upon a small number of
friends of the same sex is usual, and a great deal of imitative
and social learning occurs from friends, family, relatives, and
society at large.

To some extent the 'sexual divide' that this creates is a bad
thing, as evidenced by the tensions of the Feb Lib movement in
the last few decades, resulting in many people increasingly
taking sides more and more openly and strongly in the War of
the Sexes.

One regrettable result is divorce rates circa 50% in many
advanced Western economies, one of the saddest and most
destructive signs of their growing decadence and decline.

Perhaps, therefore, there should be more emphasis now on bringing up children with a belief that they are first and foremost people and that, whether they are boys or girls is of secondary importance.

Whichever sex they are, their goal should be at least a comfortable and satisfying life as far as possible on both the family and the work fronts, understanding that a family should never involve feelings of sexual bias of any kind, but rather should involve *sharing* resources and experiences.

Girls and their toys

Girls, of course, are supposed to be 'nice' and look accordingly. Thus they are dressed in bright colours such as pink to look 'soft' and 'girly.' They are taught from an early age to look after their appearance by brushing their hair, keeping clean, and avoiding injury.

From a very early age they are given dolls, and later dollhouses to play with, obviously with a somewhat 'training for life' intent.

Their bedrooms are often carefully decorated and furnished to look 'girly' using colours such as pink, frilly curtains, bedspreads with motifs such as flowers, and often having some sort of 'vanity unit' for themselves to practice the arts of self-beautification.

Thus girls are brought up to be narcissistic and thence self-indulgent and spoilt. So they soon learn to act like spoilt brats who throw tantrums to demand whatever they want at whim, withdrawing into a "I'm not going to talk to you" huff when they can't get their way or are upset by anything, even something relatively innocent that may have been said to them.

As one writer said: "Women are very unforgiving," and this, indeed, is certainly a trait they learn young.

In the last couple of decades in particular, however, a substantial proportion of women take up sports such as boxing that were once strictly male ones.

Others go into higher management, and others into politics, areas in which they generally seek to behave in a more manly and professional manner.

Boys and their toys

Boys on the other hand, as that absurd rhyme goes, are supposed to be made of 'puppy dogs tails' and so forth (an absurd and revolting idea). That is, they are supposed to be 'rougher.'

So they are brought up from an early age with toy guns, toy tools, balls and so forth. They are encouraged to indulge in silly and dangerous pastimes such as skateboarding and BMX bike racing, no doubt preparing them to drive like idiots and hoons when they grow up.

Before very long they are playing absurd and animalistic games like rugby, so obviously a training to 'obey orders blindly' and charge the enemy on command, and thus a preparation for war.

In this sort of way, indeed, our society has developed that sort of 'decadence disease' that saw the fall of the Roman Empire. Not long ago, for example, shops and pubs were closed on Sundays and many people went to church. Then, some boys were choristers, as I was, like my father before me.

I hasten to add that this was in an Anglican Church and that I was not violated by any priests, though I do recall a male sixth grade teacher at the Anglican School I attended from grade four 'getting after' some of the pupils for nefarious purposes before he was eventually 'told on' and sacked.

Mentioning such matters, however, gives an additional example of how we bring children up mindlessly, if not downright criminally.

When boys grow into men they will take up booze, probably beer, a product marketed mainly as for men, drinking this in a casual, if not loutish fashion at the 'footy' and every other possible occasion to celebrate or down their sorrows, it doesn't matter which.

At the office they will wear suits related to military uniforms just to 'keep in line,' the added tie deriving historically from the scarves Roman soldiers carried to bind sword wounds.

In other words, very little of how we bring up children, whichever sex they be, makes very much practical sense.

Girls and their dogs

One 'toy' that girls seem to particularly like when they reach puberty is a pet dog and a high proportion of the people I see walking dogs in the afternoon are young girls, typically with a small, white, fluffy creature leading them.

I cannot help but think this is, in part, related to the maternal instinct, and in part a result of social imitation. In addition, these factors may affect both the young girl and her mother in making the decision to get a 'toy dog'.

I quite often also see girls in their late teens walking with both their toy dog and a boyfriend, and I usually think to myself: "She's training him" because it does look indeed that the exercise is something of a prelude to family life with children.

The whole silly business of having pet dogs began, of course, in Paris and London a couple of hundred years ago. Since then countless new breeds have been produced and having household pets is just one of many addictions of the modern consumer society that reduces us to *consumer zombies* walking the streets with a mobile phone in one hand and a cigarette or drink bottle in the other.

The pet dog, in particular, is somewhat different insofar as it can be talked to and trained somewhat, leading many people to see single women obsessed with pets as using them as a substitute for children for whom they play the role of surrogate parent.

Learning the sex roles

Many argue that the sex roles are largely learnt behaviours and Weiss and Mann (1978) cite the rearing of a normal male infant as a female. The child had lost its penis traumatically at age 7 months and a surgical sex reassignment was performed.

The child had had an identical twin brother and at age seven it was reported that "the girl likes to be dressed nicely, dislikes being dirty, loves to have her hair set, helps with the housework, plays with dolls and wants to be a doctor or teacher when she grows up. Her brother plays in the dirt, helps his father fix things, and wants to be a policeman or fireman. These children, in spite of having exactly the same genes, conform perfectly to the traditional American sex roles. Learning is evidently of great importance."

Women are winning

That boys are brought up almost from the outset to be more aggressive, and perhaps less thoughtful and careful, is perhaps a disadvantage in later life. In the old days when the office was full of men, except for the lowly secretaries, it did not matter so much how stupid they were. All the other companies were the same.

In the last decade or two, however, one notable statistic has come to light in the USA. This is that women starting up new businesses are up to three times more likely to succeed. This is an astonishing figure which I attribute in part to the fact that women traditionally do most of the shopping and are thence the main consumers. For example, they spend far more on clothes, hairdressing, and cosmetics.

Men, on the other hand, were traditionally those who knew about, bought, and drove cars. Cars are expensive both to buy and to run, especially these days, but here the picture has changed greatly and women are to be seen driving sports cars, for example, almost as often as men.

This business success statistic in favour of women probably relates to small businesses, and perhaps mostly retail or service businesses such as women's clothing, jewelry, hairdressing and beauty shops, the increasing number of natural therapies, and weight-loss studios.

In such areas 'girly' niceness, politeness, tidiness and cleanliness, and keeping things orderly are advantages. Indeed, such traits may also be of some help in the office rat race, especially if mixed with the right amount of 'girl talk' or gossip aimed at backstabbing opponents.

The bottom line, certainly, is that in a world that has always suffered too much conflict and war, too much division and hate, and too much exploitation of people, we should be encouraging men and women to adopt only those positive behaviours of the opposite sex.

The world would be a better place, for example, if men were less aggressive and assertive, and women were less haughty and vain, and all were more considerate of each other.

Conclusion

Seeing them as 'the second sex' Simone de Beauvoir used the term 'otherness' for women. This is merely terminological hot air, however, and a boy brought up by a single mother, for example, might very well be more likely to feel to be the 'other' or secondary type of person, his father having been vanquished and expelled from the family group by the mother for whatever reason.

In the West unrestrained capitalism has made it far more oligarchical than was the Roman society that Aristotle complained of as not being democratic.

Democracy is supposed to involve social equality which, of course, should involve treating men and women as equals.

I think we do need the French notion of *vive la difference.* Indeed, we need to celebrate also different people and places and their different cultures. Diverse people and cultures, however, cannot be exactly equal in any great detail, far from it. As noted in Chapter 3, men and women are physically very different, and therefore must be, to some extent at least, mentally different too, women's role of producing children, for example, being a major difference between the sexes and a life-changing one.

I would like to see girls and boys brought up in a more intelligent, practical way that prepares them for a normal and hopefully happy life. I would also like men and women that want to live in normal family life to see finding a partner for life as a life-changing event that should be considered as, perhaps, involving the most important decision of their life, that is, choosing that partner.

That choice should be made with common, agreed, objectives on the table, and without harbouring 'man vs. woman' resentments.

Then it should be realized that, particularly when the first child is born, as is probable eventually, they are a family and that membership of a family is a permanent thing.

Chapter 8

TEENAGE & SINGLE MUMS

Sex is the biggest nothing of all time.
Andy Warhol, quoted in *Halliwell's Filmgoer's Companion*,
John Walker, ed., (1997).

However, at the age of 37 he [Gandhi] *made a solemn vow,*
the vow of Brahma Charya,
the cessation of all sexual activity.
Philip Baker, *Decisions of Daring Achievers* (2004).

Sex is not all it's cracked up to be

In recent books I say that sex is God's joke on mankind (Mohr & Fear, 2015; Mohr et al. 2018). I say that because sexual intercourse, seen by most as the 'max' or peak of sexual activity, is merely an animal act of breeding, nothing more.

That we make such a big deal of disgusting acts as 'French kissing' (tongue kissing), as it was called when I was young, is compelling evidence of how incredibly stupid human beings are, and with few exceptions history proves it beyond doubt.

A friend, Tony, who claimed an IQ of 200 "tested 3 times" once said to me:

Sex is for poor people.

Question: Why?

Answer: If you have money there are better, nicer, more refined things to do such as rent a villa in Corfu for the winter months and, indeed, women like to be hoity-toity and spoilt, sugar and spice and all that sort of thing. Many of them, indeed, vote with their fannies to catch a man with money so that they can live the good life. In this sex plays second fiddle, if that, and nicer things like a private balcony at the opera, dinners in expensive restaurants or exclusive clubs, and holidays in Corfu[2], Jamaica etcetera are had instead.

In any case, the perhaps older man is probably well past the "pencil stage" as Tony called it. Tony knew all about this for, on pay days (the dole) he would hit the pubs and clubs, play the poker machines while drinking top shelf booze, and when inebriated pick up a prostitute (not hard to do if you know your way around St Kilda as he sure did) and blow the rest of his dole money trying to 'get his rocks off'.

He had serious trouble all too often because booze, of course, dilates arteries, thus redirecting blood flow somewhat, also knocking out testosterone a bit, leading to Shakespeare's celebrated lines:

> *It provokes the desire,*
> *but it takes away the performance.*
> *Therefore much drink may be said*
> *to be an equivocator with lecher.*

So drunk Tony would end up giving his last dollars to the Pro so that, one night a sympathetic Pro gave him a stack of porno magazines to perhaps save him money in future. Normally she used these to help men who'd had a few to 'get it up.'

---

[2] I once bedded a woman, then 37, me 45, who had worked for Corfu Villas, a company that rented villas to Brits wanting to escape their freezing winter. Her job was to meet them at the airport and drive them to their villa. She used to back her car onto the beach some nights and sleep there, I should imagine not alone! Now that is a bit more romantic than in the back seat of a cheap second-hand car with an 18-year old!

If Tony's sad story isn't a good example of the silliness of sex, I don't know what is.

The epidermis is the body's largest organ and I, for one, would prefer to be in a nice hotel on a tropical island with a balcony view of azure waters on a sunny day. Then I could have a lady friend give me a nice gentle back massage, though I would not need the mink glove made famous in a James Bond movie in this context.

Older and wiser now, given the choice, I would then prefer that the lady and I relaxed and chatted over a few nice drinks, rather than 'have sex.' Then if we wanted some further 'physical' thing to do a relaxed swim in the warm azure waters adjacent to the hotel would suffice, perhaps followed by a nice dinner.

The late Tony also once told me:

Sex ruins a good relationship.

Question: Why?

Answer: The answer to the last question is part of the answer here. That is, there are better things to do if you can afford either the time or the money.

A very appropriate cliché is that 'talk is cheap' but, however, this is the whole point here, namely that for we humans our uniquely complex language is what sets us apart from animals, whereas sex acts are very basic animal behaviour that can easily be viewed as distasteful.

Indeed, lack of civilized, intelligent communication has been, in part at least, the reason for mankind's seemingly endless history of tribal conflict, one that now extends to the War of the Sexes with a very high casualty rate in the West.

The bottom line is that good communication is needed for a good relationship, whatever the context.

High divorce rates and teen mums

At a time when the world (human) population is manifestly excessive it is sad to hear of teen mums being somewhat common in the USA, and certainly they are none too rare a phenomenon in Australia.

With divorce rates in such countries circa 50% the whole business of having children is precarious to say the least. For 24-hour care of young children one person is simply insufficient.

Just about as absurd as allocating one nurse to deal with a hospital room containing two patients, for example, on a 24-hour basis. Obviously she would have to try and get what sleep she could from between about 10 PM to 7 AM and the alarm buttons for the patients would have to have a fairly loud alarm connected to them.

If hospitals were organized in this way an argument could be had for only paying the nurses the same as a single mother on the dole, but I don't see that happening.

The point is that to give children the best chance in life two parents in a stable 'marital-type' relationship are needed and single mums, divorce etcetera should be avoided as far as possible.

That way the basic physical, emotional, educational and financial needs of the child are better met, and surely every child should have the best circumstances possible.

Sure, given time, there will be arguments in any relationship, especially when it involves cohabitation and thus 'space' and privacy issues. Disagreements are usually based on circumstances over a period of time, often several years, so surely they should be able to be resolved amicably given a substantial amount of time for discussion, advice from friends and family, and perhaps professional counseling.

Indeed, advice and counseling are clearly needed BEFORE getting married (or shacking up with someone), and more so before deciding to have a child, perhaps appointing someone qualified for the task to act as some sort of representative for the 'child perhaps to be.'

Then questions that might be asked include:

> Are you old enough, mature enough, and really ready to have a child and thence twenty-plus years of child care?
> Why and how did pregnancy occur? Was it planned? Was it a casual encounter? Where was it? Were you sober? How long have you known the person?
> Do you like the person and want to live with them for 20+ years? Do you think you are compatible?
> Do you think your genes are worth passing on?
> Can you afford a child?
> Where are you going to live and what will it cost?
> Do you have job? How long will it last?
> If you have not done so, should you set yourself up for a lifelong job that you like before having children?
> What do your parents and friends think of the idea of you having a child? Will they be supportive and help out?

Society is in great need of counselors to ask such questions and they should be government funded, free to all but high income earners, and GPs should be able to, and encouraged to refer women to these counselors.

Conclusion

Caro and Fox (2008) wrote:

Control over fertility is fundamental for women's quest for equity and basic human rights. The pill's ability to unshackle women from their fertility changed the very notion of the role of women in society. But it did not instantly address all those complicated issues around sex, childbearing and gender.

This statement is more concerned with feminist issues of women's rights and freedoms, however, and not with those of children.

All young women should practice contraception before considering sexual intercourse.

I say 'women' because, until the male pill has arrived, and hopefully that will be soon, 'The Pill' is the easiest and safest way of preventing pregnancy, and all pregnancies should be prevented unless they are properly planned in the sort of manner suggested in the penultimate section of this chapter.

Having a child without a partner, or with a partner one has not known for at least a few years, is foolish and will not give the child a fair chance in the rat race.

In a grossly overpopulated world with growing problems of resource depletion, desertification, pollution, global warming, evolution of new and drug resistant diseases, and growing conflict and war in increasingly crowded and ethnically diverse countries, we need to reduce human population, as China has sought to do with limited success for the last couple of decades.

To that end we need to understand that quality of life should be our priority. Thus, those without sufficient resources and support, including a long-term, if not lifelong partner, should not have children.

It is just not fair to the children.

Indeed, with something like a million children in the Third World dying of hunger each year, Tony's remark quoted earlier in this chapter, "Sex is for poor people," is all too true.

As also said earlier, better-off people have better things to do, and they plan their lives and families, and they usually have more time, more friends, and more money to help them in that planning.

Chapter 9

ARE WOMEN HIGH MAINTENANCE?

*The freedom that women were supposed to have found in the
Sixties largely boiled down to easy contraception and
abortion; things to make life easier for men, in fact.*
Julie Burchill, *Damaged Gods, "Born Again Cows"* (1986).

Introduction

As noted in the previous chapter, young girls are usually
somewhat spoilt, at least, and brought up with the notion of
'sugar and spice, and everything nice.'

In contrast boys are brought up to 'rough it' a little, no
doubt contributing, in part at least, to the greater levels of
aggression seen in young males almost from the outset.

From the beginning, therefore, we sow the seeds of
difference in their minds that two or three decades later may
contribute to their first divorce.

Women are more emotional

Women are traditionally more emotional, perhaps
something young girls pick up from the angst that the maternal
instinct gives to their mothers.

Thus, continuing on from the behaviour of infants in cots,
young girls learn to be very demanding, turning on the tears
and then perhaps sulking almost interminably when they can't
get their own way.

They throw tantrums and scream and shriek when upset, and are quick to say: "I'll tell on you" when they feel wronged by a friend at school.

This they carry into marriage and the workplace, many women being, except for the minimum 'grunt-like' communication required to acknowledge they have been spoken to, are quite uncommunicative with husbands and bosses. Nevertheless, women are very unforgiving and are excellent back stabbers when it comes to spreading vengeful and malicious gossip about husbands and bosses.

In part because of their more emotive nature, women show far more interest in psychologists and psychiatrists and often take such drugs as Valium to keep them calmer.

Women are high maintenance

In part arising from their 'spoilt brat' upbringing, and in part a cultural phenomenon, women are more demanding.

They have been brought up to believe in the fairy tale that everything must be nice, so they have to look nice and thus are prepared to stretch their financial limits by spending a lot on clothes, cosmetics, beauty treatments, weight-loss programs, and cosmetic surgery.

Then they like to have, of course, a nice house in a nice area, nice children going to nice schools, have some nice pets, and, lowest in the pecking order, a nice obedient 'lap dog' husband to 'service' them at night on demand.

In this modern age of Fem Lib they may opt to have a nice easy job part-time and send their children to day care almost from birth.

In fact, these days it would be kinder to build special maternity hospitals where children could be left a week or two after birth in a residential wing.

This could be operated along the lines of an 18th century psychiatric hospital with the children giving performances for visiting parents on weekends. That way the whole business of having children would reach the Feb Lib goal of liberating the woman.

In this scenario, of course, the woman need not get married at all, and a child would just be the result of a one-night relationship, perhaps on an expensive ocean cruise holiday.

Indeed, of course, women aspire to having the best of everything, so such a 24/7 arrangement for child care would allow them more time to spend in fancy restaurants drinking expensive wine, on shopping sprees, on overseas holidays, and visiting their psychiatrist.

Indeed, after a while it might occur to their 'shrink' that perhaps this 'high maintenance' woman is in need of a little more care and that she, indeed, should be domiciled in the funny farm, and her offspring released from it, perhaps into a government funded boarding school for the purpose.

This brave new world would probably require a socialist government and this could keep men off the streets by putting circa 25% of them in the armed services and putting the unemployed in jail and shooting them if they objected to it.

Modern women need help

In earlier pairing societies the cave or hut was the main point of production where women cared for children, cleaned up, cooked, made clothes and tended the sick. The men went hunter-gathering but, indeed, in some remote tribes the women also do most of the gathering to this day.

Modern woman, however, can't even do her own hair or even fingernails in many cases.

Next they need my business idea for the day:

JIM'S BUM WIPING SERVICE. WE COME TO YOU!

Now for women with children, especially a few of them, that would be very handy indeed.

Indeed, day care centres could outsource their bum wiping of the youngest attendees to JBWS, after all, that is the modern way of doing business and, of course, the Jims would probably be successful asylum seekers in a country rapid turning into one large lunatic asylum as a result.

Women have always relied heavily on the invisible 'apron string' that connects them to their mothers for advice, moral support and help with cooking, children and other family matters.

Women are brought up to like flowers, of course, so they often take interest in a garden if their house happens to have a worthwhile one. When it comes to things more mechanical, however, a hubby is required to mow the lawn and maintain the car and other machinery, including that in the kitchen and laundry. Hubby is also required to maintain the house and in general do the 'heavier' work, such as tree lopping, for example, should that be required.

In the old days, perhaps, marriage was more of a partnership, especially if the man was the only person in the paid workforce.

Now, however, with our standard of living constantly declining in the West, both parents have to work, two cars are thus needed, houses are more costly, and expensive day care is needed for the children.

In addition, most children live in part on junk food and mums can reduce their housework further by having take-away food for dinner a couple of times a week.

These days more and more modern mums send their children to psychologists, all too often culminating in the children being put on drugs such as Ritalin for ADHD.

Big Pharma makes big money out of such drugs, of course, yet another example of our decadent consumer zombie society, one in which it is really the competence and wisdom of the mothers and teachers that can't cope with children that is in question, and it is probably they who should be taking medication.

Conclusions

Sure women are high maintenance, a situation that increases, of course, when they have children because, naturally, children are high maintenance too.

Women's often high degree of narcissism and neuroticism comes at a considerable financial and perhaps psychological cost, however, and certainly makes them harder to live with in the long run.

Men, however, are also brought up to be half-witted consumer zombies so they follow the 'footy' and other mindless sports till death, sinking tons of beer while doing so. Alcohol is a poison, of course, but a mind numbing one in low doses. Indeed, one annoyed secretary in Germany once pointed out to me that Australians drink a lot of beer and that I should take a dose of my "medication."

As a bottom line, it is the sociological differences in the upbringing of girls and boys that contributes in part, at least, to high modern divorce rates. These are greatly exacerbated by a greedy, excessively capitalist and decadent society that is showing increasingly large social and economic cracks.

The ubiquitous political, economic and advertising bullshit that turns us into consumer zombies contributes greatly to high divorce rates because people hardly communicate meaningfully anymore, indeed, they can barely think.

Sure, husbands and wives talk to a minuscule extent over what to buy or have for dinner, often over a mobile phone. Then they can tell children to shut up and watch the 'telly' or play a PC game. All of this is only communication at animal level, however, and people just can't sit down for an hour and two and have quiet chat.

Instead, they have to have the 'telly' on, be at the footy, or be in the pub or club with drink in hand as they are subjected to raving and screaming advertisements, fans, and drinkers.

Not just women are high maintenance anymore, increasing numbers of down-and-out men being almost beyond help. And as our society regresses, so does our intelligence so that we are, indeed, into *reverse evolution* (Mohr, 2012a; Mohr & Fear, 2016; Mohr et al., 2018a).

Part of that is the increasing rate of marriage breakdown, a fundamental and large crack in society which comes at great economic and social cost to the community.

Part of the problem is an increasing 'cultural divide' between men and women, in part promoted by ubiquitous advertising that, for example, implores women to spend as much time and money as possible looking after their appearance. The invisible 'fence' that his creates is comparable to those that have always separated different tribes, different races and different religions, and led to conflict and war.

Men and women living in 'marital-type' relationships with children need to settle their differences and work in a complementary, efficient and harmonious fashion for the benefit of their children. Let the children be high maintenance, for that is at least to some extent unavoidable, especially when they are young, but physically and mentally able adults should not be so.

Chapter 10

CONSUMER ZOMBIES

*Why has advertising been singled out for this special
sermonizing? Truth is becoming more of an outcast
– kicked out of the world's many parliaments, churches,
peace conferences. Believe it or not,
the buying public likes be hypnotized by hyperbole.*
Arthur Richardson (1937).
Quoted by Robert Crawford in *But Wait, There's More,
A History of Australian Advertising*, MUP (2008).

Introduction

In Chapter Nine I have drawn attention to how girls are
often brought up somewhat spoilt so that they become
voracious consumers. Men too are *consumer zombies,* though
it is women who do most of the spending and thus are the
main targets of the increasingly ubiquitous and intrusive
advertising that we suffer in today's sick consumer society.

Whilst most ads may look stupid to many of us, they tend
to succeed in the end, in part because advertising agencies in
the US began to employ psychologists almost 100 years ago
(Eagly & Chaiken, 1993).

In the present chapter a brief introduction is given to a few
key concepts of the psychology of attitudes to give the reader
some insight into how repetitive advertising attracts our
attention and seeks to switch our attitude from perhaps
neutral, to accepting, and then favourable, at which point the
product may go on our mental shopping list.

The psychology of attitudes

Attitude can be defined as 'psychological *tendency* expressed by *evaluating* a particular entity with some degree of favour or disfavour.'

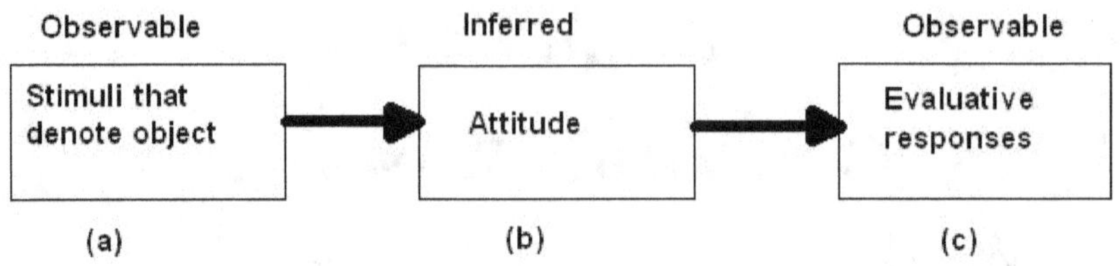

Figure 10.1. Psychological responses

Figure 10.1 illustrates the three types of response involved in attitudinal psychology. These are:

1. *Cognitive response.* This response is that of recognition of, for example, a name, a picture or other stimulus.

2. *Affective response.* This is a hypothetical construct and a latent variable. Here the sympathetic nervous system responds to (1) with feelings or emotions.

3. *Behavioural response.* This is the outward expression of (2) and may be a positive, neutral or negative response of some degree or intensity involving some observable action.

In this context conservatism, environmentalism or racism are objects. Then when we label a person a conservative, environmentalist or racist we infer an attitudinal position. Such attitudes are evidenced and also developed by the 'CAB' mechanism illustrated in Figure 10.1.

Schemas are cognitive structures that represent a person's past experience in a stimulus domain by a higher order or abstract cognitive structure. Then attitude is a subset of such a schema.

Schemas have a selective effect on the remembering of information so that people have a better remembrance of stimuli that 'fit' their schemas than for those that 'oppose.' This same selectivity applies to the 'output' of information as well as its input.

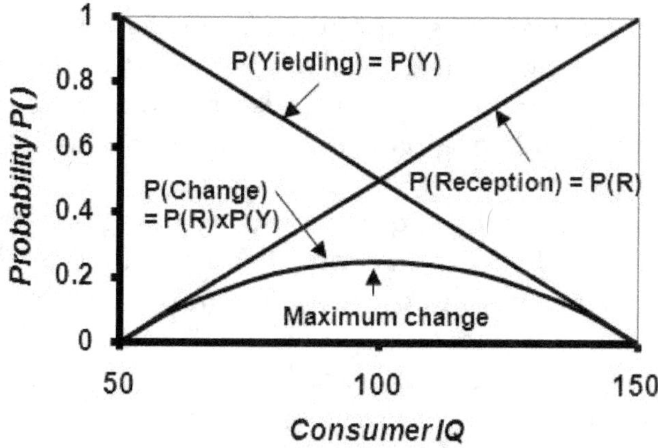

Figure 10.2. Probability of reception, yielding and attitude change.

Figure 10.2 illustrates the reception-yielding model of attitude formation (Eagly & Chaiken, 1993). Here 'reception' refers to comprehending a 'message', for example an advertisement.

This model postulates that the probability of attitude change is given by:

$$P(C) = P(R) \times P(Y)$$

so that a maximum change is obtained where the reception and yielding curves intersect, as shown in Figure 10.2.

One application of this idea is to 'get them young' so that advertising companies target the young and naive before they have the maturity or 'consumer intelligence' to develop resistance, and this is why the horizontal axis in Fig. 10.2 is labeled Consumer IQ.

The brewer's society quotation in the Sociological Differences section of Chapter 3 is an excellent example. Once an idea like 'beer is for men' is buried in a boy's brain he may become a beer drinker for life, the habit occasionally reinforced by ads that make the habit look completely appropriate.

The basic mechanism of persuasion, therefore, is to 'get them young' (and naive or 'less intelligent consumers') as Figure 10.2 suggests. To do this ads need only persuade some of the target audience and then imitative or 'social' learning ensures that many of the rest follow them.

Advertisements having achieved this, regular advertising reminds the audience of a product. Then in Figure 10.1 the 'C' response will be one of recognition of a brand, the 'A' response will be one of approval of it, and the 'B' response will be to make a mental note to buy it.

In advertising it is, of course, important to have sufficient repetitions of an ad to ensure adequate average learning by the audience.

Then, after time has elapsed after an advertisement its 'residual' effect depends upon both the *primacy* or strength of the ad compared to others, and its *recency*.

Thus repetition of ads is required to ensure long-term potentiation of the remembered message, an important objective (Vander et al., 1994). Correlation between retention and persuasion, however, is by no means guaranteed and ads can be tailored to these two ends.

Targeting advertising

Maslow defined two kinds of needs (Lindzey at al., 1978):

(a) *Basic needs* such as hunger, thirst, sex and security.

(b) *Metaneeds* such as achievement, beauty, goodness, justice, order and unity.

Maslow defined achievement as a basic need but the present author prefers to classify it as a 'higher' or more human metaneed.

First, we must meet our basic or 'animal' needs. That done we can turn our attention to the higher 'human' metaneeds and thence Maslow's 'meaning of life' goal of 'self-actualization' as a human being.

These needs provide *primary goals* that may motivate us towards *secondary goals* such as money in order to achieve them.

Most of our basic needs are *intrinsic motivations* whereas most of our metaneeds are *learned goals.*

Advertising usually targets the metaneeds of your *ego.*

A Coke ad, for example, is not designed to remind you that you may be thirsty. If so, you might rush to the fridge and grab whatever drink you can find to satisfy that thirst.

No, a Coke ad makes it look 'cool' to drink Coke with your friends and being 'cool' is a metaneed! So next day a young boy will want to be 'cool' when hanging out with his friends so they will all drink Coke and act foolishly, just like the actors in some Coke ads

Here again we see the down side of advertising, namely that increasingly ambitious executives will stop at nothing to sell their product, even if it has to brainwash the young into acquiring both bad behaviour and bad teeth.

In marketing to children, of course, familiar cuddly looking cartoon figures are often displayed on packaging and used to speak the lines of TV ads. Here, however, ads usually target the *Id,* the basic 'animal' personality that has basic needs like hunger. Young children tend to eat in smaller doses and often so that almost any time they are awake is a good one to put a picture of confectionery in front of them.

One of the best examples of brainwashing, however, is the use of *consumer panels* of children in marketing research. The children are often asked what they will say and do to persuade parents to buy them the product.

Finally, the extent to which children are exposed to advertising is incredible: - - "*it is estimated that children between 2 and 11 years old may see over 20,000 advertisements in a year,*" (O'Guinn et al., 2006).

Advertising, therefore, will persuade someone in your family, even if it doesn't persuade you!

In marketing to adults well known sporting identities are often used to market such things as golf clubs, household appliances and cars and houses. Indeed, this was the basis of Mark McCormack's very successful IMG (McCormack, 1986) and one of his earliest clients was Greg Norman who, marketed as 'The Shark', was made out to be a much better golfer than he was and Norman made an awful lot of money from TV ads.

Types of advertising

Some marketing campaigns use *push strategies* which concentrate on the availability of products. In this case the ads are 'basic' and concentrate on telling you the product name and where to get it. Examples of such ads on TV are:

➤ A presenter reads a script while holding the product in question up in front of the camera.
➤ Ads with only text messages and a voice-over.
➤ Semi-humorous ads which sometimes use cartoon characters to present their message.
➤ Ads targeting children which involve cuddly characters and fantasy scenes.
➤ Ads for junk food which play on having a high 'reward/effort' ratio (Govoni et al., 1988). That more than 50 million people a day eat McDonald's stuff is testament enough to the success of their advertising.
➤ Ads where the reader just about screams at you not to miss some bargain sale or to go to some cheap store.

Advertisements for 'basic' food, junk food, confectionery, clothing and home appliances are usually of the 'push' type.

Marketing campaigns often use *pull strategies* which promote the product in order to attract buyers. In this case the ads concentrate on 'image' to attract the audience to the product and the product name is secondary and *associated* with the imagery.

Examples of this sort of ad on TV are:

➤ Sophisticated ads that show the product in 'classy' surroundings with actors dressed stylishly.

➤ "Laid back' ads were the presenter extols the virtue of the product with, for example, an island resort as a backdrop.

➤ Ads that use glamorous people such as movie stars as actors.

This type of advertising is usually used for higher priced or more 'up market' products, including fashion clothing, cosmetics, expensive furniture, luxury cars, and overseas holidays.

One of the most important 'levers' in advertising, undoubtedly, is *keeping up with the Jones's*. This is exploited heavily in marketing cars and new gadgets of which the mobile phone is the supreme example at present.

Another powerful inducement is selling on the 'never-never', for example with no repayments for a year.

The ubiquitousness of advertising

Today advertising is literally everywhere. On TV in Australia there used to be regulations limiting the amount of advertisements per hour to something bearable. Now there seem like 20 minutes or more of ads per hour at times. Worse still, owing to the increasing cost of TV advertising time, a truly bewildering string of ads appears in each ad break, sometimes ten of them.

It is almost as bad on radio where there are sometimes as many as half a dozen ads at once on the higher rating commercial stations.

Junk mail from supermarkets and other retail chains has reached epidemic proportions. Other 'direct marketing' is done by phone and is increasingly irritating, often involving requests to complete lengthy market research surveys over the phone.

In addition, free local papers almost totally full of advertisements are also stuffed into millions of letterboxes in major cities.

Trams, trains and buses carry plenty of ads, as do train stations and tram and bus stops.

Taxis and trucks all carry signage, as do many vehicles belonging to small businesses.

Shopping strips are becoming more and more cluttered with advertising signs above the shops, and sandwich boards and often products on the footpath.

More and more restaurants, coffee shops and juice bars have also spilled out onto footpaths, sometimes making little room for the pedestrians for which they were originally intended.

Shopping malls are filled with advertising and more and more stalls with spruikers have appeared in them.

Sporting grounds carry more and more advertising and sporting teams now carry prominent advertising on their clothing.

Casual clothing often comes complete with the brand name writ large upon it.

The Internet is full of advertising, of course, some of it of a lurid nature.

Then there is the despicable practice of placing confectionery and soft drinks near the checkouts at supermarkets, resulting in many a tantrum as young children taken shopping throw a tantrum to get another dose of perhaps the first 'drug' of addiction, sugar.

Perhaps the most predatory advertiser of all, Coca Cola, has its vending machines just about everywhere, including pubs and clubs, office buildings, stations and heaven knows where else (they are probably there too!).

New trends in marketing

Many of the new trends of late involve products aimed at improving our health:

1. Healthy foods, for example low fat products.
2. Organic foods.
3. Pollution free and environmentally friendly products.
4. Diets and weight watching.
5. Alternative therapies. Of these the list grows daily:
     Aromatherapy.
     Herbal remedies.
     Acupuncture and Chinese medicine.
     Group therapy.
     Exercise therapy, for example Yoga and Pilates.
     Transcendental meditation.
     Reflexology.
6. Vitamins and other dietary supplements.
7. Weight loss programs and fitness equipment.

In many large cities where house prices have tended to become unaffordable to new entrants to the market there is a growing 'live for today' approach to consumer spending and this is seen in:

1. The growing fast food industry, including take-away food and packaged 'heat only' meals sold in grocery stores.
2. Increasing diversity in consumption of alcohol.
3. Increasing use of drugs which may perhaps be encouraged by the legalization of marijuana.
4. Increasing use of leisure industries such as gambling.
5. Increasing use of restaurants, pubs and clubs.
6. Greater spending by young and independent working women on cosmetics, clothes, jewelry and other beauty and fashion products.
7. Greater spending on magazines, videos, books, computer games, music and other home entertainment products.
8. Greater spending on major items like cars and holidays.

In these and many other areas there seems to be a growing market which advertisers are busy exploiting, encouraging gullible women consumers to indulge in "retail therapy."

Conclusion

The extent to which modern marketing intrudes in our lives has almost reached saturation point with rafts of a dozen TV ads at a time, free local papers almost full of ads, highly irritating telemarketing, dishonest 'not really cheaper' door to door marketing of retail energy supplies, and almost daily junk mail filling our letterboxes.

Rampant capitalism has thrived on the massive, almost exponential growth in human population since the Industrial Revolution in Europe and now we have had further industrial revolutions occurring in massively populated China and India.

The results have been increasing resource depletion, pollution, desertification, evolution of new diseases, and climate change, threatening our long-term survival (Mohr, 2012c).

In the meantime, we have been reduced to *consumer zombies* and, in fact, our intelligence is decreasing so that we are, indeed, now in *reverse evolution* (Mohr, 2012a; Mohr & Fear, 2016; Mohr et al., 2018a).

Chapter 11

BOSSY WOMEN, EMASCULATED MEN

Women can't forgive failure.
Anton Chekov, *The Seagull,* act 2 (1896).

*I think women are just as aggressive as men but it's
suppressed in us. With men it's totally out of proportion.*
Lesley of 'Silverfish', quoted in *The Whole Woman,*
Germaine Greer (1999).

*The first time I took testosterone, I felt truly liberated
I'm delighted that my voice is deeper and I have a subtle
difference in the way my muscles form.
My sex drive has increased . . .*
Janet 'Texas' Scanlon, quoted in *The Whole Woman.*

Women are winning

There is no doubt that women are winning the War of the Sexes gradually. They got the vote long ago, generally they have equal pay, and more and more women are finding their way into higher management and politics.

In the West, as manufacturing continues to move offshore to find cheap labour, traditional men's jobs continue to disappear whilst more and more traditional women's jobs in teaching, day care, social work, secretarial work, reception, office management etcetera are appearing. Thus a sign of the times is a new Australian TV series *House Husbands.*

If women are to rise above men in society at large that will, of course, take more than a generation or two, but the progress to date has been comparatively rapid in historical terms.

As for getting 'on top' in a heterosexual marriage, a article in 'The Age' newspaper on July 5, 2012, reported that feminist activist Jaclyn Friedman called for "mainstream narratives inviting us to identify with women who like to dominate in bed . . . women of colour and queer women as sexual heroines in control of their choices."

Bossy bitches

Unless brought up in poverty, girls tend to be somewhat spoilt, having to have 'everything nice' etcetera. Often girls have a 'toy dog' or cat as a pet and can get in some early practice at 'control' over this.

When they have children and the maternal instinct goes into overdrive they become, more often than not, control freaks. As a mother they now have a considerable increase in status and have control over a husband and at least one child.

In the age of Fem Lib, however, they have even more power and often literally dominate and oppress husbands who they reduce to virtual slaves. When the woman starts back at work the husband now only brings home *part* of the family income, a very different situation from being the sole breadwinner.

Indeed, in seeking to advance themselves in the workforce many women 'masculate' themselves, for example by wearing suits that are, by and large, a feminine version of men's suits. Then, in line with the key objective of Feb Lib, they try to emasculate male opponents, including their husband, as far as possible, most obviously by being more 'butch' than they are.

In my one marriage (with two children) my wife, who I had thought from the outset was a bit butch, was a bossy bully to the extreme and ultimately ruined my career and life.

The next woman I lived with I offered half of a house I lived in that was divided into two good sized flats. I suggested only nominal rent but she paid nothing until I asked for some money after receiving nothing for about eight months.

At the outset, however, she insisted that her flat have new carpet throughout and be painted. This I did at great expense, getting some help from one of her two sons with the painting. Then, when I asked her whether her son could help do a little painting in my flat, she said flatly: "No, that's your side."

One rule for the bossy bitch, another for the oppressed and cheated man.

A few years ago, impatient about delay in publishing a paper in an Australian Maths journal, I was a little rude in a fax to a woman editor of the journal. To my complete surprise she sent the police to visit me. Translate that to an office scenario and you have female staff calling the cops whenever they feel somebody has not been polite.

Subsequently I was never able to get a reply to further enquiries about the paper and it was never published in the end, proving that it was the bossy woman that was the crook, not me.

Traditionally women often used to speak of men taking advantage of them, the usual context being in matters of sex. These days, if a man is in a relatively lowly and subordinate position in the workplace or at home, or both, then women will take advantage of it and be rude and domineering, and I have experienced this with women many times. In other words, we really do live increasingly by the law of the jungle once more as we sink deeper into *reverse evolution*.

Prohibition

Prohibition in the USA in the first half of the last century was, of course, brought about by the women's lobby largely because then, of course, it was men who did most of the drinking. Indeed, in Australia up until the middle of the 1970s pubs typically had a main bar which was for men only and a small back bar for women which was little used.

In those days it was thought that women should not drink much, perhaps in part because, having less muscle and being smaller, they only metabolize alcohol at about half the rate men do on average. Another reason might have been that lower class pubs were pretty 'rough' places full of inebriated men and foul language near closing time, and were thus thought not fit places for women to be in.

Another factor is that men do need a good deal more dietary calories and booze helped provide them when, probably, they ate much the same amount as their wives. Often too, the wives being the cooks and having more access to food, they would get increasingly fat as they grew older, perhaps making hubby more inclined to seek refuge in the pub.

These days, with an obesity epidemic sweeping the West, more and more people are becoming grossly obese, the majority of them women who pass this trait on to their children through epigenic marking.

With Feb Lib having been increasingly active and effective since the 1970s, however, women are drinking more and more, as evidenced by the increasing numbers of women being caught for drink-driving, often with very high readings.

In Australia in the old days lower class women drank only sherry occasionally, but now there is a wide range of drinks marketed at women, ranging from colourful mixed drinks such as 'Vodka cruisers' aimed at young women to champagne and chardonnay aimed at older women.

Myself, I have met two full-blown female alcoholics, both with connections to political parties.

One of them was press secretary to a Minister in an ALP government in Victoria. His office had porn movie sessions when he was busy in the House and the press secretary had one lonely male child, had little food in the house, and rented a spare room to an alcoholic journalist who she could drink and chat with and ignore the child.

The other I met at a Liberal Party meeting and she worked from the flat she lived in as a hairdresser. Again I could see little sign of food in the house!

Lie your way to the top

Women are the ultimate liars, of course. For example, try asking a woman you have just met about her past love life and you are unlikely to hear anything like the whole truth. Similarly, you will rarely hear a woman admitting to doing anything of significance wrong because they are very good at blaming others for anything that goes wrong.

In addition, women pride themselves on being big talkers and, indeed, they often are and take every opportunity to lie and backstab people when gossiping about them.

The first thing to beware of, of course, is people who can't open up to you, for you can assume that they will open up about you to other people.

Myself, for example, I had a bossy backstabbing wife that sometimes would tell others what I had done or was worried about lately in front of me, and that, of course, was just the tip of the iceberg full of BS she would spread about me.

One lady friend of mine for a year or so was an accomplished liar. For example, buying a cheap second-hand car which was far from legally roadworthy she talked the dealer into giving her a roadworthy certificate. As she told me later, the dealer said: "I don't know why I'm doing this."

In other words, women are also good at getting people to lie for them. My ex-wife, for example, having never been able to talk to or consult with me about anything, told me she had written fourteen pages about me for the lawyer she used for divorce proceedings. I never saw or heard any of the lies in those 14 pages which was, of course, both unfair and dishonest.

Butch women

It was the early 1970s when jeans became fashionable in Australia and soon women were able to look more masculine by wearing them. Now, of course, we have fat-arsed grannies still wearing them and looking truly ugly and stupid.

Now too we have more and more women 'getting on top' and dominating and the feminine literature reflects this. For example, the top selling book *Fifty Shades of Grey* about a virginal female student's relationship with a rich man who likes bondage and being dominated is said to be in the genre "clit-lit", another indication of the *reverse evolution* that we are now undergoing.

In addition more and more women are taking up male pursuits, a more extreme example being boxing:

I recently gave my best mate Iva a black eye when aiming for her arm. Fisticuffs are a normal part of our drunken bonding sessions. Emily Sheffield, woman boxer.

If follows, of course, that lesbianism is on the rise also as, of course, that way at least one woman can 'get on top' or they can take it in turns, perhaps using a dildo or vibrator. As the world's human population is at least twice that sustainable for the long term, however, at least one could hope that butch and lesbian women will not have children. Nevertheless, some of them do adopt children, however bizarre that seems to sane people.

Abusive and violent women

From an early age girls learn to turn on tantrums and unleash streams of abuse when they are upset by the smallest thing.

I once had a University secretary say: "You bastard" when I had her type a letter to a colleague in another country including the sentence: "I can't get anyone to lick a stamp here." The point is that, in my whole time in that University I never heard anyone else swear. Sure they were sometimes rude or nasty in other ways, sometimes extremely so, but it took a woman to swear at me.

As for violence:

Even then radical women were demanding the right to aggression as a basic human right and women's groups were training in self-defence and martial arts (Greer, 1999).

I once had my wife threaten me in the kitchen with a large knife and she was extremely threatening in doing so. True there had been an altercation a couple of nights previously, but by pulling a knife on me she had raised things to a new level.

Once a lady friend objected to me renting a spare room to another female. Visiting one day she thought the tenant was revealing too much cleavage and forced her onto the floor and, sitting astride her, began to pull her hair out, only stopping and leaving when I called the police.

Once I was playing a tape of King's College Choir at a lady friend's house and she said that I was playing rubbish.

I blurted out: "You'd fuck donkeys wouldn't you."

After that she could not stop hitting my face and I had to, with difficulty, catch a taxi home covered in blood.

As a young child of about six my mother was once about to take to me with a steel dog chain, presumably because I had used a rude word, probably merely a 'language experiment' at that age. She was only prevented by my father saying: "Don't do that, you'll hurt the child."

Regarding the last two incidents, the bottom line that we all need to be aware of is that a sudden remark can incite a rapid instinctive defensive reaction because it is seen as a threat, this before the brain has had time to evaluate the 'threat' rationally. Indeed, pro footballers use sudden rude remarks to 'get opponents in.'

A final example, I once had two women police come to my door telling me there had been complaints about me ringing a certain (overseas) phone number. I mumbled defensively and apologetically, whereupon one of the cops exclaimed forcefully: "Don't dick me around!"

Whether the two policewomen were dykes I don't know, but it seems quite likely. They certainly were 'partners' in crime on that occasion at least.

Lazy, selfish women

These days women are lazy compared to the 'old days'.

Now they hardly have to cook thanks to the huge range of frozen, tinned and packet food available.

In addition, of course, there is a plethora of take-away food available, some of it with the option of home delivery for a small extra charge.

Finally, there is now a huge range of snack foods and confectionary available to help 'fill the family.'

Unfortunately, processed foods are full of additives, many of them harmful and perhaps carcinogenic, and have also lost much of their nutritional value. Some also contain traces of substances that may be allergenic.

Thus we not only have an obesity epidemic in the West, but in some places there appear to be epidemics of allergenic ailments. In Barbados, for example, 20% of the population suffers from asthma and there are 10 times as many hospital admissions for this as there used to be.

Another growing problem is high intake of high GI foods in children, contributing to a growing incidence of ADHD.

On the food and diet issue my now ex-wife was always careless, at best, giving no thought whatsoever to nutrition and simply whacking whatever was quick and convenient on the table and always keeping plenty of ice cream in the fridge to keep children quiet.

Almost without exception women I had much to do with after my divorce were even lazier. One woman I rented a next door flat to for the best part of a year hardly bought food at all that I can recall.

Instead, she had to go out and get takeaway food. Thus when a cousin of hers visited occasionally she always had to raid my fairly substantial food stocks to give him a meal.

In 'marital-type' relationships these days, of course, the man is expected to do far more around the house. Statistics suggest that the woman still does more of the housework, but slowly this is changing.

Conclusions

Women have always been inclined to be bossy and self-righteous, in part being brought up that way.

Now, however, they are more arrogant, selfish, dishonest, lazy, self-indulgent, narcissistic, self-opinionated, and intolerable control freaks than ever.

Men, however, are just as thoughtless and stupid as being 'the stronger sex' once allowed them to be.

As noted in following chapters, with women taking over the education system and entering higher management and politics in ever higher numbers, however, women are certainly beginning to win the War of the Sexes.

Chapter 12

HOMOSEXUALITY

*In addition to the normal sexual urge in men and women,
Nature in her sovereign mood had endowed at birth certain
male and female individuals with the homosexual urge.*
Karoly Benkert, Hungarian Physician, 1869.
One of the first uses of the term 'homosexual'.
Quoted by Colin Spencer in *Homosexuality: A History* (1995).

*I will resist the efforts of some to obtain
government endorsement of homosexuality.*
Ronald Reagan, remark August 18, 1984.

*At the same time, British writer Julie Burchill came out in
The Sunday Times – after having left her husband for a woman
and then left that woman for her brother - -.*
Elizabeth Wurtzel, *Bitch, In Praise of Difficult Women*,
Quartet Books, London 1998.

Introduction

Amongst the most disturbing indications of the corruption and decadence in our society are the all too frequent reports of sexual abuse of children by priests, teachers and relatives. It seems that even the once most trusted people in our society can't be trusted any longer.

Sex, of course, is ubiquitous in our increasingly depraved society. Brothels were once illegal back street affairs. Now sex chat lines are widely advertised on late night TV, a pathetic attempt to shield children from it, and brothels are advertised in free local newspapers which children of all ages collect from the letterbox after coming home from school.

A fundamental change is that homosexuality is on the increase. Once a trait one had to keep secret, it is now rampantly displayed at gay Mardi Gras festivals, at gay bars in major cities, and in late night TV ads for homosexual dating services.

Homosexuality

Some claim that homosexuality is inherited and a study of 113 people in 33 families in which at least two brothers were homosexual found a genetic marker on the X-chromosome (Xq28) that had a very high correlation with sexual orientation (Galton, 2001).

Genes may play a minor 'predisposory' role but, largely, homosexuality is a learnt behaviour. Typically, for example, the normal heterosexual male has one or two homosexual experiences in adolescence (Robertson, 1981), and no doubt the same applies to women.

Those who become homosexuals, therefore, presumably do so as a result of imitative learning at an early age.

Thus the earliest sexual experiences of children begin with self-exploration, learning that girls and boys have different sexual organs, and chat about sex and perhaps 'show me yours' with same-sex friends.

Next might come observation of more extrovert children at school indulging in masturbation, and then perhaps involvement in relatively innocent and mild homosexual acts with a friend.

There are, no doubt, also psychological factors involved, for example a lack of confidence in approaching the opposite sex coupled with the fact that there are earlier homosexual experiences to draw upon as an alternative behaviour model.

If alcoholism is to be regarded as a psychiatric illness, as it often is (Davies, 1971), then in my view homosexuality is even more obviously a treatable psychiatric condition as well.

That said, most of our heterosexual behaviours are also learnt ones, many of them hardly natural or healthy.

A seemingly innocent example might be what was called 'French kissing' in my youth, that is what can be described as 'tongue kissing', a truly revolting and very unhealthy practice like many other modern sexual practices.

The bottom line on sex, though, might well be that if we were aiming to get any smarter and wiser then abstinence might be the wiser course, especially as a sound exercise regime is clearly a healthier option. Obviously, however, quite the opposite is happening, all part of our *reverse evolution.*

Poofters

Homosexuality is still more common amongst males, and the main derogatory Australian term for a male homosexual was poofter, and it was widely and frequently used until relatively recently.

Myself I see hints of homosexuality in male urinals that allow men to 'perv' over each other's private parts and, indeed, even celebrities have been caught out in the USA by police stings when trying to pick up someone in public male toilets.

Similarly, I am suspicious of the small heated pools that British soccer teams jump into together after a match.

Likewise, of course, there is the common row of 'open' showers in men's changing rooms at sporting venues, again providing plenty of opportunity for team members to indulge in a little male sexual bonding.

Then there are the armed services where men without women have often indulged in homosexual practices, a splendid example being TE Lawrence dedicating his epic book *The Seven Pillars of Wisdom* to a young Arab boy he had been in love with. Indeed, in the book he describes how the desert soldiers he commanded often strolled out into the dunes with a partner to "slake their thirst" for sex.

Indeed, one cannot help but think that under such circumstances male homosexuality must have been a relatively common thing, perhaps involving circa 5 or 10% of men to some degree, at least.

'Butch' women

In part encouraged by Fem Lib, there is no doubt that women have tended, en masse, to become more 'butch'. In part participation in male dominated areas of the workforce must have almost forced them to become more dominant:

Though Margaret Thatcher was at least as bellicose as any male head of a western democracy, and thousands of women have fought under the aegis of the military-industrial complex, the feminist struggle against violence continues. (Greer, 1999).

Women have also taken up traditionally male sporting pursuits such as football and boxing:

I recently gave my best mate Iva a black eye when aiming for her arm. Fisticuffs are a normal part of our drunken bonding sessions, Emily Sheffield, woman boxer.

It seems likely that such changes in women's behaviour, and particularly the publicity given to them, have contributed to an increase in homosexuality in women.

In addition, of course, such events as gay festivals and marches have greatly contributed to this increase.

Lesbians

Anne Lister, who lived in the first half of the 18th century, is now a famous lesbian thanks to discovery and translation of her copious diaries hidden in the family estate of a homosexual relative, John Lister, in the 1960s. The diaries, all 4 million words of them, had been written in code, but were finally published in the 1980s (*The Real Story of Anne Lister*, ABC1 TV, 12.30 AM 13/3/2012).

Anne was sent to an exclusive girls school and became a lesbian at 13 when consigned to sleep in an attic because she was deemed a nuisance. There she began a relationship with an Indian girl also banished to the attic.

Ultimately, the Indian girl was committed to an insane asylum for life.

Anne seduced many women, having met many of them at a church, her diaries mentioning her great sexual appetite and experiences.

One of Anne's earlier affairs lasted 3 years, but then the other woman married a wealthy man, but her lesbian relationship with Anne continued sporadically through weekends spent together in hotels. Anne grew manlier over the years, her figure became less feminine, and she even grew a moustache and a beard. This eventually caused the illicit relationship to end.

Anne's love life was saved by inheriting the family estate and she seduced a wealthy local heiress who she married and lived with.

Eventually a male business competitor began to criticize Anne's relationship with her 'wife' publicly and, finally, Anne died when infected by a tic while on a tour of Russia.

That her memoirs were finally published in the 1980s, at the point when the modern, sometimes radical, Feb Lib movement had been acquiring considerable influence, must have added a little more support to its cause.

Indeed, feminists began to argue against heterosexuality, thus encouraging lesbianism.

For example, according to Bryson (1992):

> ➤ *"For some, the issue was not simply one of sexual pleasure, for heterosexuality itself was declared to be a 'political' institution rather than a natural expression of sexual desire."*
> ➤ Radical feminists argue that 'politically correct' sexual activity precludes sex with men, viewing it as an act of oppression, domination and rape.

> A 1970 book by Anna Koedt claimed that female sexual pleasure came from the clitoris and thus did not require penile penetration.

Little wonder, then, that homosexuality is on the increase both amongst men and women.

Conclusion

Not long ago society was such that women needed men not only to have children, but also for financial support and physical protection.

Indeed, physical protection was more necessary in our troglodyte days when 'shacking up' as family groups was the only option. Still, however, we praise those who die in our still ongoing wars for having protected our way of life, and thence families and children. Now that our way of life in some Western countries is so decadent, however, one wonders whether it is worth protecting and, indeed, many millions of more extremist Muslims are in no doubt that God should eliminate such decadence.

As for homosexuality, the increasing pressure to legalize gay marriage makes me wonder when people will next want to marry their dogs. They would probably have both better looking and more intelligent offspring that way, so long as they married dogs of the opposite sex, that is, and that is perhaps doubtful. 'Gay', I guess, means being free of offspring, however, so perhaps people wanting to marry a dog would still want a same-sex marriage.

Chapter 13

FREUDIAN WOMEN: BAD MAD & SAD MAD

Women's lives have become more, not less, difficult.
They are better lives, but they are harder.
If it could be shown that women have reason to be sad,
they might be spared the stigma of being mad.
Germaine Greer, *The Whole Woman* (1999).

A mad world

Some have long said that it's a mad world but that could never be truer than now. With our population having exponentiated since the Industrial Revolution in Europe, and with decadence now afflicting mankind more than ever, things have never been so bad. George Bernard Shaw, for example, famously said: *"An asylum for the insane would be empty in America."*

Thanks to continuing wars, terrorism, economic crises, overpopulation, and overgrown megacities real standards of living are falling in the supposedly advanced economies.

Now we are subjected to ubiquitous and ceaseless marketing by transnational companies to the point at which we have ended up *consumer zombies* shuffling around wearing uncomfortable jeans with a mobile phone in one hand and a cigarette or drink bottle in the other (Mohr, 2012a; Mohr & Fear, 2016; Mohr et al., 2018a). One direct result is that more and more children are addicted to high GI foods and thus are diagnosed with ADHD and put on medication.

Mad women

The biggest name in psychiatry, of course, is Sigmund Freud, detested today by many women because he and Jung associated most mental disorders with women, presumably because most of their patients were women, but also because of such statements as Freud's clanger:

> *The only bodily organ which is really regarded as inferior is the atrophied penis, a girl's clitoris.*

'The Dissection of the Psychical Personality, *New Introductory Lectures on Psychoanalysis* (1933), Lecture 31.

Freud and his colleagues, of course, were obsessed with such absurd notions as penis envy and the Oedipus complex. Little wonder then that Hitler at al. had his books burned, his Jewishness no doubt being another motivation:

What progress we are making. In the Middle Ages they would have burned me. Now they are content with burning my books. Letter by Freud to Ernest Jones (1933) referring to the public burning of his books in Berlin.

While such pioneers as Freud and Jung associated most psychiatric disorders such as hysteria and depression with women, it would seem that none other than Germaine Greer (1999) agrees with them:

The evidence seems to be that it is getting worse. Thirty years ago we heard nothing about panic attacks, or anorexia or self-mutilation. Now the ikons of female suffering are all around us; the image of the battered woman is high fashion. The models reeling down the catwalks are stick thin, their faces cavernous and bruised, their hair matted. Scars and bruises are conspicuously worn. Hollow-eyed model girls seem to be saying: "if I am to be hurt I must be hurt." Lacking others prepared to injure them, it seems, they will hurt themselves.

It is true, however, that women seen to more emotional, in part it is often claimed because men tend to hide, if not bury, their feelings. Nevertheless, women being more emotional is a source of prejudice against them:

Faced with a choice between a male or a female candidate, for example, many voters unreflectively vote "male" on the grounds women are too emotional – jittery, flighty, high-strung – to steer the ship. Tong (1998).

In contradiction of this, however, Feb Libbers always trumpet that men are more aggressive, if not violent, but this is usually the result of anger, itself an emotion. Indeed, it is emotive, even hysterical outbursts by women that shock men into responses that may sometimes be violent. Thus a female verbal assault which may be quite prolonged and thus disturbing may result in a physical response by a male partner, an oft-repeated scenario in the War of the Sexes.

Sad mad

I like to make the simple but useful, indeed important, distinction between *sad mad* and *bad mad.*

One way in which many women experience a range of symptoms is premenstrual syndrome which often causes fatigue, headaches, irritability and depression and in more serious cases may require treatment with hormonal supplements, aldosterone antagonists, or simply oral contraceptives (Davies, 1971).

In addition, mild depressive symptoms are often seen in early pregnancy, particularly when the pregnancy is unwanted (Davies, 1971).

My view is that with the world overpopulated and 50% divorce rates in many countries, termination of any unwanted pregnancy should be considered by assessing the woman's psychiatric state, family situation, resources, and ability to deal with the child adequately if the pregnancy is allowed to go to term.

In addition psychiatric symptoms occur after 30% of pregnancies, including depression which is sometimes severe, and also schizophrenia, and may require professional treatment (Davies, 1971).

Finally, the climacteric period around the onset of menopause causes physical and psychiatric symptoms in up to 70% of women. The physical symptoms may include 'hot flushes', headaches, arthralgia, hypertension, diabetes and obesity. The psychiatric symptoms may include depression, anxiety, obsessive behaviour, hysteria and paranoia. Hormone replacement therapy with oestrogens is often used to treat such symptoms (Davies, 1971).

Other psychiatric problems in the sad category that may affect women more than men include anxiety, for example over the physical and mental health of themselves or their children, and obsessive behaviours, for example being somewhat manic about cleanliness.

Bad mad

Psychopaths dominate the bad mad class of people, and the pathology of their condition may include abnormally aggressive or irresponsible behaviour, delinquency, aberrant sexual behaviour, and extreme dishonesty.

Thus most tycoons fall into this category because they usually cheat the system somehow to get rich, particularly CEOs who seem obsessed with increasing their salary and bonus packages, often while presiding over company crashes which they escape with the traditional 'golden parachute' and laugh all the way to the bank while leaving thousands of lowly workers and pensioners bereft of their life savings.

True, most of these have been men to date, but plenty of women are joining the ranks of upper management and some of them are proving even more crooked than the men.

Psychopaths, of course, like to bully people as well as cheat them, and women are extremely good at bullying.

With children, for example, they often become extreme control freaks, as one can often see when they are yelling at their children in the street or the supermarket.

Women are also exceedingly good, if not compulsive, liars. They can do no wrong, almost, if they are to be believed, and I have met quite a few women who combine excessive assertiveness, bossiness, bullying and lying in various degrees.

Many women also have a hysterical personality:

The hysterical personality is a term applicable to persons who are vain and egocentric, who display labile and excitable but shallow affectivity, whose dramatic attention seeking and histrionic behaviour may be to the extreme of untruthfulness, who are very conscious of sex, sexually provocative, yet frigid and who are dependently demanding in interpersonal situations (Chodoff & Lyons, 1958).

Case studies

In chronological order cases I have seen include:

➢ My wife (now ex) was a superlative bully, liar and backstabber. It was a disastrous marriage: our backgrounds had nothing in common and our experience, intelligence and personality differed greatly. For a few years she secretly took Valium and predictably, she ruined my career and life.

➢ A woman I knew briefly had been left on the shelf at 35 and was a sad case. She was committed briefly when neighbours in her block of flats heard her screaming loudly and lived on medication.

➢ An absurdly bossy woman I knew for a couple of years made me spend half my meager savings renovating a flat I was renting to her. She paid no rent for 8 months until I asked for the nominal amount owing. She belonged to a women's group aimed at empowering women and once said: *"Women are going to take over the world."*

- ➢ A woman I knew for a couple of years I met by renting her a flat in the other half of a biggish house I lived in alone. She had been committed to a private psychiatric institution after being sacked from her chief executive job. She turned up in a white lab coat saying she was a diet consultant at the institution. In fact, she hardly bought any food, lived on take away food, and never paid any rent or for constant use of my phone.

- ➢ Another woman I rented that 'half house' to suffered extreme anxiety. She had lived for a few years with a member of a rock band, saying he had given her "a hard time." Once when a visiting friend said outside the house something along the lines: "You've forgotten to take your medication" the woman exploded with anger and put on a tantrum which could be heard for quite a distance. A few months after she moved to live with her rather spooky mother she broke both legs when hit by a car. I immediately wondered if it was an accident.

- ➢ A woman I met only a few years ago had just about every psychiatric condition most can think of. She blamed it all on a disastrous marriage to a Maori slaughterman who she said had hit her and then kicked her in the head when she had fallen to the floor. She OCD and anxiety, both closely related of course, along with some degree of depression, some degree of schizophrenia, and was borderline morbidly obese. A major factor in her condition was having had a fall at age 53 while working her own cleaning business. This damaged her back and she had not been able to work since. At 65+, having lived alone for more than 2 decades, and been without an occupation for about a decade, were perhaps the major factors in her condition, for which she took about 20 pills a day, half a dozen of them for psychiatric purposes.

Conclusion

Women clearly seem more prone to mental problems, in no small part related to their sexuality and thus menstruation, menopause, stress of pregnancy, and anxiety over child care.

Men, however, seem naturally more aggressive, physically at least, and they even look it usually. Women on the other hand can be much more aggressive verbally.

The distinction between *sad mad* and *bad mad* I think important, the former category often deserving of sympathy, the latter category usually warranting condemnation.

Mohr's Tenth Law is that one usually should judge things out of 10, not just as black and white, and certainly the severity of madness should be rated, for example catatonic schizophrenia might score 9/10, whereas occasional depression might only rate about 1/10 (Mohr & Fear, 2015, Mohr et al., 2018).

Chapter 14

JOBS FOR MEN
DISAPPEARING FAST

Although the absolute number of jobs in American manufacturing was rather constant at about 17 million from 1969 to 2002, manufacturing's share of jobs continued to decline from about 28% in 1962 to only 9% in 2011.
Blog by Gary Becker and Richard Posner, 22/4/2012.

5% of the working age population of Australia
[is employed in the manufacturing industries in Australia]
Manufacturing Statistics Australia bulletin, June 2011.

Introduction

Thanks largely industrial revolutions in China, India and North Korea being kick-started by globalization, and the greed for profits via cheap labour, manufacturing has declined dramatically in the USA, Australia and like countries.

Except for the garment industry, which in Australia largely went offshore to Asia circa 40 years ago, most of the lost jobs have been traditionally those for men.

In addition mechanization has been gradually reducing the size of the workforce in many industries since the early days of the industrial revolution in Europe nearly 300 years ago, again most of the jobs lost being those of men since, of course, the workforce was traditionally largely made up of men while most women minded households and children.

Mechanization

James Hargreaves, who had worked as a carpenter and hand-loom weaver in Blackburn, Lancashire, was asked by his employer to make an improved machine for carding wool (untangling the fibres) in their raw state. Observing an ordinary spinning wheel he hit upon the idea of a spinning jenny which could spin several threads at once. His first spinning jenny was made in 1764 (Odle, 1966).

In 1768 a mob of angry cotton labourers gutted Hargreaves' house and destroyed his machinery. He moved to Nottingham and, with a partner, took out a patent for his machine in 1770.

In 1769 Richard Arkwright took out a patent for a horse-powered spinning-frame. In 1775 he patented a carding machine and made other machines for drawing and roving cotton, reducing it to thinner strands for feeding to the spinning-machine.

In 1789 a mob smashed up his mill but he continued his work regardless and in 1790 he applied steam power to his spinning frames. In that same year he heard that a mob was about to march on his Derbyshire mills and organized a battery of guns and issued 1500 small arms and 500 spears to all able-bodied men in his employ. The would-be attackers dispersed before reaching any of his mills.

Since those early days of the industrial revolution in Europe the march of the machines into manufacturing industries has met with little resistance.

Now large machines have largely replaced man on modern farms, whilst robots have replaced a good many of the workforce in such industries as the car industry.

New technology, including open cut mining, has also considerably reduced the size of the workforce in the mining industry

The result has been a considerable reduction in the number of jobs available in many industries, most of their workforce having been men.

Cheap offshore labour

Unable to compete with cheap labour in Asia, much of manufacturing in the USA, Europe, and Australasia has disappeared. In the USA the GFC required the government to bail out GM and Chrysler, whilst in Australia GM and Ford remain only thanks to government support.

Many service industries have also gone offshore, for example many telemarketing operations are now based in India.

In Australia Quantas Airlines has moved much of its operations offshore to cut costs, such changes bringing occasional calls to lower the minimum wage in Australia.

It is for such reasons that we have been led to accept that a headline unemployment statistic of 5% is OK. In fact this is just the usual econobabble that economists feed ignorant politicians to spout at us.

As Marx pointed out, keeping such a large pool of unemployed simply helps keep the wages of those still working down (Sweezy, 1946).

With our real standard of living having fallen considerably in the West in recent decades, we can only fear that 10% headline unemployment will before long become the norm, with a great many more people than that in only part-time work, on disability allowances, or having given up looking for work and retired early.

Cutting middle management

With the considerable growth of many transnational companies in recent decades their hierarchical trees have grown in height and breadth, in part as a result of duplication of middle management positions in different countries.

In the last decade or so many large companies have pruned their mostly male middle management considerably, CEOs giving themselves even more astronomical salaries in self-congratulation for any savings.

In addition, of course, more and more women are replacing men in middle management as they seek to break the glass ceiling much deplored by Feb Libbers.

Women taking over

Women are not only taking what were once men's jobs in middle management, they are also moving into higher management and politics in increasing numbers, as noted in Chapter 17.

As pointed out in Chapter 16, women have also taken over much of the education system, displacing most male teachers in schools and many others in tertiary education.

In addition, most of the new businesses being started are mainly staffed by and their products made for women, examples being the still growing beauty, fitness, alternative therapy, and child care industries.

This is in part the reason for a startling statistic that appeared in the USA a few years ago, this being that in starting new businesses women were about three times more likely to succeed than were men.

Economic decline of Western economies

For the last two decades there have been occasional mass protests in the USA against globalization and the local jobs being lost as a result of it.

With the 2008 GFC matters simply became worse whilst the current EFC in Europe seems likely to affect a few countries, at least, for a decade or more.

With China's economy having slowed a good deal, and expected by many pundits to slow further, that will probably contribute to economic slowdown in countries such as Australia and Brazil who supply China with much of its raw materials for manufacturing.

Thus the long-term outlook for employment is not good and, in fact, it is likely that we shall have to become used to higher levels of unemployment.

Conclusion

It does indeed seem that women are beginning to win the War of the Sexes, to some extent at least, and the new hit TV series in Australia *House Husbands* is surely a sign of this.

Not only are new job opportunities and businesses for women appearing, but occupations traditionally dominated by women such as nursing continue to grow as our society becomes more stressed, new diseases appear, incidence of others such as cancer increase, and an epidemic of obesity and diabetes sweeps many advanced countries.

Finally, with the US economy still struggling, and some countries in Europe struggling to prevent economic collapse, more and more men's jobs are in peril.

With our population at least twice that which is sustainable for the long term with any comfort, we can only expect unemployment to increase and, indeed, may have to look to countries like Cuba, which has no unemployment or homelessness, for ideas on how to deal with the situation.

Chapter 15

CREATING MORE JOBS
FOR WOMEN

*In Australia, 76 per cent of women
in the 45-54 age group are in paid work,
compared with 52 per cent 20 years ago
Australian Bureau of Statistics finding, 2005.*

Introduction

As Greer notes (1999) it was in part because so many men were killed or crippled in wars in the 20th century that women began to enter the workforce in greater numbers:

Squandering of men's lives in foreign wars resulted in more women entering the workforce but most working women duplicated outside the home the functions carried out by women in the home. Thus secretaries played a mothering role to their male employer, not only by playing receptionist and typing his letters but also by playing the role of advisor, protector from disturbance, and laying on tea and coffee and cleaning the office.

Many of these secretaries were in the armed services and war also brought more nurses into the workforce too, and many female cooks and cleaners as well.

In addition, the increasing numbers of women at work needed more services such as child care, further increasing the number of women in the workforce.

Office work

Traditionally receptionists, secretaries, and typists have been women, and sometimes in smaller businesses all three roles are combined.

With the advent of the PC their role has changed somewhat but, if anything, has become even more important.

In addition new office-based tasks such as telemarketing have become popular and created many new jobs which are mostly filled by women.

As for the advancement of women, many a secretary has managed to take the eye of their boss and end up marrying him.

Shops

In the last century, in particular, women have increasingly taken over the 'over the counter' role in small shops and now as salespersons and cashiers in banks, supermarkets and most retail businesses.

In addition, there are increasing numbers of businesses aimed at women including fashion clothing, hairdressing, manicurists, beauty parlours, weight-loss centres, tanning studios, natural therapies and flower shops.

Nursing

Nurses were once always women and that is still largely the case. The health industry has, however, expanded greatly in the last century or two.

This is in part because cures have been found for many diseases, and also because many new diseases have been recognized, particularly in the mental health area.

In addition, modern technologies such as cars, electrical appliances, and power tools have provided new ways in which we can injure ourselves, adding to the queues for treatment in hospitals.

The aged care industry

With life expectancy having increased considerably the aged care industry has grown enormously and this, of course, employs mostly women.

Natural therapies

There is an ever growing number of natural health therapy businesses mostly run by women for women customers. These include herbal therapies, aromatherapy, reflexology, physiotherapy and massage.

Other health businesses such as acupuncture are increasingly being operated by women.

The childcare industry

With more and more women forced to work to help pay the rent or mortgage, and pay for new 'gadgets' like the second car, huge TV, mobile phones etcetera, women paid well enough must have pre-school children looked after in the childcare industry.

Thus they use their *competitive advantage* of higher pay than that of childcare workers to have their children minded while they are at work.

In many cases, however, by the time the substantial child care costs are added to the sundry costs such as commuting there is very little money left over after tax to contribute to the household income. Thus women with two or more children are less likely to use childcare whilst single mothers often opt to live on government welfare payments.

Social work

Not very long ago social workers were few and far between. Their numbers have increased enormously in recent decades. Now qualifications up to degree level are required, further increasing employment in the sector.

Conclusion

Only a few examples of the many areas that mainly employ women have been considered here. Others include community facilities such as libraries, child health centres, youth centres, and function centres.

In addition, increasing numbers of women are entering traditionally male areas of employment ranging from management to mining.

In Australia more women now study at University than men so that women are beginning to dominate some professions such as dentistry and teaching.

With changes in Western society such as people having smaller families, more and more women entered the workforce, a trend which increased after Word War 2 during which the male workforce was decimated.

Thus in the USA the greatest growth in workforce participation has been amongst both women and Hispanics (Robbins, 1994), the proportion of white non-Hispanic males in the workforce dropping below 40% for the first time.

The greater number of women in the workforce has, of course, had an economic multiplier effect and thus created many further 'flow on' jobs for women, for example in day care centres.

In addition, working women are more likely to go to a hairdresser regularly, feed the family on takeaway food regularly, have a cleaner to clean their house regularly, and also perhaps have a lawn mowing service to clean up their garden occasionally.

Busy women are also more likely to be stressed and use the services of psychologists for themselves or their children, in part the reason for an epidemic in ADHD supposedly affecting our children and a sad symptom of our increasingly decadent society.

Chapter 16

WOMEN TAKING OVER THE EDUCATION SYSTEM

Whereas a rattle is a suitable occupation
for infant children, education serves
as a rattle for young people when older.
Aristotle, Politics bk 8 (1340 BC).

The childcare industry

The takeover of the education system by women begins with the childcare industry which, with the entry of more and more women into the workforce, has expanded enormously.

Only two or three decades ago the only preschool education was in kindergartens and in Australia, as elsewhere, a minority of children went to these, and then only for the year before starting school. In addition, many children went to kindergarten for only a few hours a week.

Now, however, some children are locked in day care centres for 10 or more hours a day for 5 days of the week.

Like kindergartens, day care centres are always run by women but the latter sometimes employ the occasional male. These are relatively easy or 'soft' jobs compared to most others, particularly as there is often a high degree of job security, if not almost a guaranteed job for life.

In day care centres, however, very little worthwhile education takes place. Instead, the children are merely kept amused with games, stories, videos of children's cartoons, let out into a small playground frequently to relieve their boredom slightly, and made to sleep once or twice a day.

Not long ago many people, if not most, would have regarded such incarceration of pre-school age children as cruel. Furthermore, the heavy dosage of lightweight 'kids stuff' and 'monkey stuff' in the playground may do more harm than good educationally and, in fact, put them behind children given more attention by intelligent mothers at home.

For example, Weiss and Mann (1978) refer to a project in Milwaukee that found that children given more attention by the mother or a specially trained teacher, showed markedly higher IQ. This is no doubt the reason that only children tend to have higher IQ and that, in families with more than one child, the eldest child has a slightly higher IQ on average (Vernon, 1960).

School

The early years at school were always dominated by women teachers and still are. In those early years things are taken very slowly, in fact too slowly. Indeed, 12 years at school is too long and 10 years would be a more sensible norm.

This could be achieved by condensing the first 8 years of school to 6, an easily achievable result as most children learn little more than the 'Three Rs' in this period.

In addition, the best students could still be 'tracked' and thus enabled to complete their schooling in 8 or 9 years. This would be consistent with the fact that Leonardo da Vinci was apprenticed at age 14. Indeed, Francis Bacon *left* Cambridge University at 14, having completed two years of the three-year Tripos.

In Leonardo da Vinci's case it was his father who noticed that he seemed to have some artistic ability at an early age, an example of how the sometimes more ambitious thinking of men can produce better educational outcomes.

In contrast, the slow and tedious rote learning that dominates most years at school, if not those in higher education as well, tends to stifle creativity.

Indeed, the author recalls that, while he was doing his PhD at Cambridge University, the Australian UG students at Churchill College had a barbecue at which he noticed a small sign stuck to a bottle of fruit juice called *regurgitation juice*.

Declining academic standards

A survey of 24,000 students in twelve countries by the Educational Testing Service in Princeton found that, compared to 40% of US students scoring at the 500 level in a standard test, the results were 78% for Korea, 73% for Quebec and 69% for British Columbia (Sykes, 1995). A similar decline in standards has occurred in Australia.

In the USA outcome based education (OBE) has gone a long way towards disallowing fail grades, instead allowing students to retake tests until they pass. The idea of this is to avoid attaching negative labels to students, and much effort is also made to avoid attaching positive labels to the brightest students as well.

Similarly, OBE eschews 'tracking' to permit accelerated learning for gifted students, despite conclusive evidence of its positive results, in this way ensuring that the overall standard of education is lowered further.

In the USA new 'soft' approaches to teaching and grading reading and maths have led to a dramatic decline in literacy and numeracy skills.

It is women teachers, in particular, that favour these soft approaches to teaching that are reducing real standards.

Indeed, in part this may be the reason for the decline in IQ seen in the UK (Vernon, 1960) and the USA (Mohr, 2012a; Mohr & Fear, 2016; Mohr et al., 2018a) in the last century.

In addition, women are far more inclined to be dependent on psychological and psychiatric services, including for their children and, in the case of women teachers, their students.

The overlong school education system should bore anyone with half a brain. To make matters worse increasing numbers of 'unruly' children are diagnosed with such doubtful disorders as Attention Deficit Hyperactivity Disorder (ADHD) and prescribed drugs such as Ritalin to sedate them:

By 2004, in the UK, prescriptions for Ritalin and similar drugs had risen to 360,000 - - double the level prescribed in 1999 – and this is only one type of stimulant drug given to children (Holford, 2008).

In the USA and Australia in turn, increasingly large numbers of children suffer this fate. Reports of up to 15% or more children in some areas being on such drugs have not brought action to curb this disturbing trend as yet, but visions of a future society in which both parents and children have to be drugged to cope are unacceptable.

Regrettably, it is usually boys who are diagnosed with ADHD, no doubt because they are inclined to be a little more active and energetic both physically and mentally than girls.

Indeed, this reflects a growing bias in the education system and elsewhere in society, much of it owing to feminine liberationist ideology. Thus, unfortunately, women teachers will tend to favour girl students, a situation that needs to be redressed urgently.

Another problem is that today's young, thanks to better nutrition, grow faster than in the past. Leonardo da Vinci observed that children were half their ultimate height at age three. Now that figure is about 55%. Along with that, in part because of the ubiquitous media today, in many ways they mature faster than ever before.

Many children by their mid-teens, therefore, are becoming bored with school and drop out, particularly males these days.

Technical colleges

Technical colleges originally trained for 'hands on' occupations such as carpentry, plumbing, and electrical services installation and maintenance. Then they began to teach slightly shorter diploma courses in Engineering.

Eventually many of these courses were lengthened to match those in Universities and ultimately these colleges were rebadged as latter day and lightweight Universities.

The original trade courses remained in TAFE colleges which in some cases split off from the original technical colleges. In the last decade or two these TAFE colleges have expanded their range of courses enormously, including such courses as hospitality, cooking and management. Now some TAFE colleges run degree courses and even some masters degree courses.

The result, much of it resulting from an increasing presence of women in TAFE as both staff and students, has been a massive increase in the number of institutions giving diplomas and degrees and, of course, in the number of people receiving them.

Indeed, the situation has become absurd as most further education courses are now in areas in which training was once only by apprenticeship, or in areas in which little or no formal training was once required.

16. Women Taking Over the Education System

Universities

Not very long ago very few women went to University and only about 100 years ago Cambridge University did not allow either women students or staff.

Now, however, there are more women students at Australian Universities than men. Thus, of course, there are now many more women staff in Universities.

Correspondingly, there are more courses that are mainly undertaken by women, for example nursing which was once largely learnt by apprenticeship in hospitals.

Now women school teachers greatly outnumber men and teacher training is now dominated by women who have overseen a considerable reduction in standards.

Sykes (1995) reports widespread disillusionment with modern teacher training, much of which is a hotchpotch of psychology, sociology and history that cannot develop real expertise in any of these areas.

He cites several examples of recent doctorates in education being granted for dissertations with such titles as:

"The use of goal setting and positive self-modeling to enhance self-efficiency and performance for the basketball free-throw shot" for a PhD at the University of Maryland.

After such largely useless studies, Sykes laments, 'educrats' move into educational administration and oversee a decline in standards over the whole spectrum of education comparable to that evidenced by their largely irrelevant doctoral studies.

Women have also overseen an excessive growth in ridiculous University courses, for example Masters Degrees in Sexology and Puppetry at two Australian Universities.

In addition, MBAs are now so common that with an MBA one might now only be able to gain employment as a salesperson, if that.

Once upon a time correspondence courses were poorly regarded. We are such slaves to fashion now that the morons in Universities are happy to run courses by *distance education* over the Internet.

Such changes have been overseen by an overgrown educational bureaucracy. In the US in 1960 one third of education employees were not classroom teachers. By 1991 46.7% were non-teaching staff and the teaching staff's share of the total payroll had shrunk from 54% to 41%. Much the same has occurred in England and Australia both in school and tertiary education.

The bottom line is that Universities have become so profit oriented that the highly paid educrats that run them will stoop to anything to grow their institution, prostituting themselves by kowtowing to fee-paying overseas students to improve the bottom line. Consistent with their concern with 'bottoms,' all that remains is for Universities to run courses in bum wiping, perhaps as a post-diploma in nursing.

Conclusions

Women have always dominated the pre-school education system and they now run the greatly expanded day care system. They still dominate the early years of schooling and have largely displaced male teachers in the later years of schooling.

Unfortunately, one reason for this are the occasional scandals about child sex abuse by male teachers, particularly in Catholic schools but also in other schools proclaiming a religious ethic. The hypocrisy of the church, of course, knows no bounds, and people wont to worship false Gods cannot be expected to be anything but queer, if not downright loony.

This has helped women displace most male teachers in school but now, however, women teachers too are being caught out indulging in sex with their students, perhaps leveling this disgusting playing field somewhat.

This gives parents even more reason to consider home schooling, in addition to both the excessive number of years of largely rote learning at school and the falling standards.

In fact, Penn (2007) reported that increasing numbers of children in the USA are schooled at home.

Though only 2 percent of children are home-schooled at present, home-schooled children made up 12 per cent of the finalists in the National Spelling Bee. In three out of seven years home-schooled students also won the National Geography Bee.

In 2001 a home-schooled boy in Montana finished high school at age 15. Not feeling ready for college he wrote a novel that became a best seller and was made into a movie.

The bottom line is that, in part thanks to being dominated by women, the education business has grown out of all proportion. Twelve years at school is too long, let alone a few more in day care centres, and then countless years can be wasted studying such ludicrous courses as postgraduate diplomas in Sexology and Puppetry.

It is not surprising, therefore, that over 50 years ago it was found that average IQ in the UK had decreased and continuing decline was predicted (Vernon, 1960). Recent studies confirm that this *reverse evolution* is actually happening globally.

Chapter 17

WOMEN MOVING INTO MANAGEMENT & POLITICS

If you want to run for public office, you could be elected,"
Bill told her.
"But I've got to go home. That's just who I am."
Conversation between Bill and Hillary Clinton
Elizabeth Wurtzel, *Bitch, In Praise of Difficult Women,*
Quartet Books, London 1998.

I owe nothing to Women's Lib.
Margaret Thatcher, quoted in *Observer* (London, 1 Dec. 1974).

Introduction

Women were always really the boss of the household, an important role. At best husbands pitched in and helped a little, at worst they ignored domestic matters and children largely. In the latter instance the husband might have said often: "What's for dinner?" or some such, a little like a customer in a restaurant, but his wife was running that restaurant and he was the customer who, of course, paid for it.

In the office the secretaries were always women, of course, but this placed them close to management. Often, indeed, the result was some degree of extra-curricular involvement with the boss, an example being the affair between Jim Cairns, a popular member of the Australian Government in the 1970s, with his secretary, an affair which led to his resignation.

In business similar affairs were not uncommon and sometimes businessmen married their secretaries.

With changes in Western society such as people having smaller families, more and more women entered the workforce, a trend which increased after Word War 2 during which the male workforce was decimated.

With the Feminine Liberation movement strengthening a good deal over the last four or five decades, more and more women have moved into management.

In Australia, for example, more women now study at University than men, so that we can expect a further increase in the number of women in management, particularly as there are already a significant number of women CEOs to encourage that increase.

In politics the global scene now includes a significant number of women, some of them in high positions. In Australia circa 20 percent of the members of the Federal Parliament are women and this number is rising.

Moving into management

Women have moved into all levels of management in significant numbers but, of course, there is always some resistance to change of which Caro and Fox (2008) cite an example:

When she was told her application for the position [as a junior product manager] *had been successful, she was also sternly warned that one person strongly objected to her getting the job. "This person is much more important to us than you are," she was told, "so it is your job to win her over." The person who so strongly objected to having a woman in a management position (albeit the most junior such position imaginable) was the CEO's secretary.*

Kipnis (2007) notes that the feminist movement's drive for equal pay for women has backfired to some extent because highly paid men have sometimes been replaced with lower paid women. She adds:

All proceeds from economic growth and increases in productivity were kicked upstairs, to the top 1 percent of households (who managed to acquire 57.5 percent of corporate wealth by 2003); the middle classes saw no gains at all. In fact, the wealth of every group other than the top 1 percent has declined since 1991. Hey, where's the equity in that?

She goes on to point out that changes in tax policies helped top CEO salaries rise to 1000 times the average pay, and that the average pay for the average US worker would be much less if they were not now working an extra 160 hours a year, that is, about 3 hours more per week.

High and sometimes enormous executive salaries are, of course, a strong incentive to the ambitious to climb the executive ladder and many women have done so.

Indeed, women being greater consumers than men and being more inclined to like 'nice' and often expensive things, that perhaps adds to their motivation to earn more money. In contrast most men are brought up more prepared to rough it, for example getting dirty playing football in the mud, and thus many are still prepared to spend their lives working as lowly paid slaves just as most men always have.

A key factor helping women rise in the workforce hierarchy is that traditionally Human Resource Management (HRM) departments have usually been run by women, presumably an extension of their traditional secretarial and receptionist roles. Thus, of course, they have ample opportunity to promote the cause of women job applicants.

Women's businesses

A great many businesses produce products for women, for example the cosmetics industry, beauty parlours, hairdressing salons, manicurists, fashion clothing stores, naturopaths, and weight loss studios.

In such businesses, therefore, it is wise to have at least a few women in management positions and, indeed, women have often started and run such businesses themselves with considerable success.

This may be one reason, along with the fact that women are the principal consumers in society, that in the USA it was found that women were three times more likely to succeed in starting a business than a man.

An important industry in which women play a major role is that of publishing, most magazine and book publishing being for the women's market, including children's books of which women are, of course, the main purchasers.

Thus many publishing organizations are largely run by women, giving them much opportunity to influence public opinion, and to influence it in favour of women's interests and causes.

Women in politics

Not that long ago women did not have the vote. Now that about 50 per cent of the voting public are women many of them, if not a majority, will be inclined to vote for a female candidate whenever possible.

The Westminster system of parliamentary democracy dates back to the 13th century and change in such venerable institutions takes time. Slowly, however, more and more women are becoming involved in politics at various levels from the grass roots of local branch meetings right up the being leader of the government.

In addition, women often assume leadership of important unions which have considerable political influence, for example the powerful teachers and health workers unions.

As communicators it is sometimes argued that men, being naturally more aggressive, use communication to emphasize their independence and status in the hierarchical social order, whereas women use communication to establish connection and empathy (Robbins, 1994).

Such an argument could be based on the behaviour of primates, male gorillas thumping their chests to show their power whilst the females sit in groups minding their young.

This greater ability of women to seek connection and empathy could, if it was clearly directed towards the lower paid working majority, help them to succeed in politics.

As for different leadership style, Robbins (1994) states:

Women are more likely to encourage participation, share power and information, and attempt to enhance followers' self-worth. They lead through inclusion and rely on their charisma, expertise, contacts, and interpersonal skills to influence others. Women tend to use transformational leadership, motivating others by transforming their self-interest into goals of the organization.

Men are more likely to use a directive, command-and-control style. They rely on the formal authority of their position for their influence base. Men use transactional leadership, handing out rewards for good work and punishment for bad.

In summary, it might be said that men tend to have a more autocratic leadership style and certainly our memories of such people as Hitler and Stalin would support that view.

Women, on the other hand, might be said to have a more democratic leadership style and this might favour their political prospects at a time in history when monarchies have become irrelevant, the power of the church has decreased greatly, and when people in several countries are still struggling to overthrow dictatorial or authoritarian regimes.

As always, Germaine Greer's attention-seeking views are over the top:

Though Margaret Thatcher was at least as bellicose as any male head of a western democracy, and thousands of women have fought under the aegis of the military-industrial complex, the feminist struggle against violence continues. In The Female Eunuch I argued that feminism would have to address the problem of male violence both spontaneous and institutionalized, but I could suggest no way of doing this beyond refusing to act as the warrior's reward. Even then radical women were demanding the right to aggression as a basic human right and women's groups were training in self-defence and martial arts (Greer, 1999).

In Australia when we had a woman as deputy Prime Minister for the first time she did a pretty good job of backstabbing the PM and taking over his job.

After a couple of years, with an election just a year away, her women colleagues began a concerted character assassination program on the (male) opposition leader, this based on his supposedly being sexist and so forth.

Indeed it is very noticeable now that women in politics and management tend to stick together on feminist lines, taking politics and business to new lows in which the feminist lust for power and control overrides the interests of the community at large. So much for that supposed caring capacity of women!

Conclusion

Women are entering higher levels of management and politics in ever increasing numbers.

Indeed, as a simple exercise in arithmetic, in the progressive West (to the point now of extreme decadence) we might expect more nearly 50% of our political representatives to be women before long.

As for women wanting their own independent say in politics, I remember well that my mother used to vote the opposite way to my father at election time and, indeed, my ex-wife also voted in opposition to me.

Women, of course, tend to have slightly different concerns. In Australia, for example, it is women more than men who are attracted to the Greens Party, perhaps in line with their traditional caring role in families.

Finally, it is my view, however prejudicial that it may seem to some people, that women are much better liars than men. That, at least, should stand them good stead in politics!

One woman I knew had not finished school and had only done a few months of a low-level commercial studies course. Nevertheless she managed to land a role in middle management as an accountant and I well remember her telling me how she used to 'bone up' from a book in the lavatory to learn the rudiments of her job.

That reminds me of Frank Abagnale Jr, immortalized in the movie *The Great Imposter* starring Tony Curtis and based on Abagnale's memoir *Catch Me If You Can*. The movie was remade with the latter title a couple of decades later with Leonardo di Caprio playing Abagnale.

Chapter 18

THE FASHION, BEAUTY & SEX INDUSTRIES

*Women's power inheres in our bodies,
our childbearing capabilities, our female sensuality
– all of which terrify men and society.*
Laura Kipnis, *The Female Thing,
Dirt, Sex, Envy, Vulnerability* (2007).

*I don't think a prostitute is more moral than a wife,
but they are doing the same thing.*
Prince Philip, Duke of Edinburgh
Observer (Dec. 1988), quoted in *Sayings of the Eighties*
(Jeffrey Care ed., 1989).

The fashion business

There is some logic in bracketing the beauty, fashion and sex industries in this chapter because models parading down a catwalk are not inherently different from prostitutes in bright clothing standing on sidewalks in red light districts: both are showing off to buyers of the products and services they sell.

Similarly, a woman who goes to a lot of trouble with her makeup and clothing is doing so to make herself look attractive. The prostitute on the sidewalk, perhaps in a red dress, is doing likewise.

The woman, however, is probably acting for sociological reasons that have become habit and, perhaps, made her somewhat narcissistic.

The prostitute's story, however, is often a sad one of drug addiction and thence a need for money. Worse still, some young girls are forced into the sex trade by bad circumstances.

The bottom line is that the beauty, fashion and sex industries are all about making money from the brainwashed consumer zombies of our decadent societies.

The fashion industry, of course, is often somewhat absurd, if not extremely so. They way in which men, and then women, have been sold on the idea of wearing uncomfortable jeans once intended only for (male) farm workers in the USA is beyond belief.

Now, indeed, we have fat-arsed grannies still looking stupid in them whilst young girls pay ridiculous prices to buy jeans cut off to make short pants with ragged edges which make them look quite insane.

The high end of fashion is even more insane and simply vanity gone mad with rich women paying exorbitant prices to show off their wealth.

The beauty business

Women in some primitive tribes go to great, if not absurd, lengths to make themselves look 'interesting', for example stretching their necks with increasing numbers of hoops, or their lower lips with small plates.

Not much has changed with time. Not long ago women used to almost crush themselves in incredibly tight corsets to ensure a shapely figure.

Even now women still almost cripple themselves in high or even stiletto-heeled shoes, pierce their ears to hold ear rings, shave their legs, have bikini waxes, and pluck their eyebrows

Then they paint their finger and even toenails, paint their lips thickly with lipstick, and cover their faces with face powder to hide even the slightest blemish.

All this, of course, is a huge multinational business more to do with making money for a few than doing any favours to the suckers from whom they make money.

Not long ago women did their own hair and took pride in ornate brushes they kept for the purpose. Now they spend increasing amounts of money having their hair and perhaps nails done in salons.

Many working women would argue that they don't have time to do their own hair, at least not well. Similarly, however, they farm out their children to day care, sometimes almost from birth, and perhaps need help with housekeeping, shopping, cooking and so forth.

All this so they can have an often menial job such as in a day care centre, a job which would not exist if people such as they stayed at home to look after a household and family. Indeed, the stress of their now complicated lives is, of course, a major factor in the high divorce rates in the increasingly decadent West.

The beauty business is much encouraged, of course, by countless women's magazines that implore women to emulate the glamorous women pictured in them in order to capture hunks like the well-known male film stars whose love and family lives are often discussed on a regular basis.

The weight-loss industry

This too is big business now that we have an obesity and thence diabetes epidemic in the West. Indeed, not only do many women go to a women's gym a couple of times a week to try and lose weight, they often sign up to programs that provide prepared meals on their doorstep designed to help them watch their weight.

Part of all this are the late-night infomercials on TV that advertise fitness equipment to give both men and women nice 'abs' and a good figure.

Then there are, of course, a great many women's magazines devoted to the issue of cooking and diet to help weight-watchers.

There are also many magazines devoted to the issue of fitness and body building, most of these for men.

The publishing industry

One of the most profitable areas of publishing is the 'romance business,' the Mills and Boon books being a prime example. For the book publishing industry books on romance are amongst the most profitable and numerous and are mainly written by and for women.

The magazine industry also produces a wide range of women's magazines which focus on fashion, beauty and gossip about the love-lives of internationally famous people or well-known local ones.

Then there are many soft-porn magazines amongst which Playboy might be regarded as a pioneer of the 'tit parade.' These have grown more absurd over the years, for example the magazine 'Jugs' which is full of pictures of usually older somewhat fat women with big, fat boobs.

In the USA romance fiction is a $B1.2 industry, much smaller than the porno industry's $B9 turnover (Kipnis, 2007), but the two are not very fair comparisons, as these figures related to romance books, whereas the porn industry is mainly magazines, many of which are monthly, some by subscription.

Sex shops

In Australia, at least, sex shops only sell to people over 18 years of age. Their product range begins with a wide range of magazines, mostly more explicit and heavily pornographic than can be legally sold elsewhere.

They also have a wide range or pornographic videos which, I presume, show plenty of tits, arses and sexual organs along with sexual acts and perhaps group sex. Some of these, I believe, women call 'stick movies.'

More amusingly they sell dildos and vibrators, some of them truly massive.

According to Kipnis (2007), vibrators are a godsend:

Thankfully for the worn-out doctors, the electrical vibrator was invented in the late 1880s, reducing the labor involved from hours to far more efficient sessions, often producing multiple orgasms, and reducing the fatigue factor on the part of the physician. The medical practice of genital massage may have faded out by the 1920s, but the female orgasm was no less of a social problem.

Another woman writer said that she had a small vibrator that she called 'the pocket rocket' and which she found useful when her car was stuck at the traffic lights.

Also aimed at women's pleasure, in part at least, are vacuum devices supposed with frequent use to enlarge the penis.

Then, I suspect, there must be range of body lotions, massage oils, and lubricants for the act of sexual intercourse.

Finally, I'm sure sex shops carry a range of prophylactic devices which might include small pumps for inserting prophylactic creams before intercourse, diaphragms, and condoms in various weird shapes, colours and sizes.

In reality, however, having looked briefly out of curiosity a couple of times, I find sex shops comparable to a House of Horrors by way of their affect on me.

Phone sex

Phone sex is one of the most remarkable, and insane, products of modern times. That it is advertised so frequently on late-night TV amazes me.

So far as I have seen this is usually aimed at men and what men get out of, or rather what they do perhaps, while listening to a few expensive minutes of sexy talk on the phone I can only imagine, as no doubt can intrepid readers of this book.

I suppose there must be sex chat lines for women, however, just as there are male and female phone numbers for dating services also advertised on late-night TV.

Indeed, there are sometimes late TV ads for homosexual chat lines. Those I have noticed to date are for men, but surely now there must be such services for lesbians also.

Sex chat lines are not a far call from prostitution and, indeed, such chat is often a key part of a prostitute's way of working to help the clients 'get it up.'

It would not surprise me, therefore, if some sex chat line calls ended with the phone number for a brothel, or indeed for a particular prostitute being given to the caller.

Prostitution

It is often said that prostitution was the first profession but I believe the first profession was that of witch doctor, that is a person professing belief in spirits or Gods and claiming that by contact with them he could cure sickness.

Indeed, in primitive tribes without even money it is difficult to imagine prostitution.

Some time after the Agricultural Revolution, circa 10,000 years ago, it is easier to imagine, and it is very easy to imagine in Rome 2,000 years ago.

The second of the quotations that opens this chapter is typical of the foot in the mouth stuff that Prince Philip was noted for until he reached old age. There may have been some truth in it when few wives were in the workforce and women could be viewed as wanting to seduce a man using sex to catch him and keep him as breadwinner for a family.

One of the most famous brothels in history was Madam Kitty's pleasure palace in Berlin (Blundell, 1982).

Its clientele included many of the elite from Germany's diplomatic corps and armed forces. In 1940 it was taken over by the Nazi central security organization, the SD, and all the rooms wired to five monitoring desks in the cellar.

During that year 20 girls worked around the clock to 'service' 10,000 people and in one month 3,000 sessions were recorded. One result was that the Spanish foreign minister, taken to the brothel by his German counterpart, was heard to reveal a Spanish plan to occupy Gibraltar and the plan was able to be squashed by the Germans.

A few years ago *The Times* of London reported that an Austrian ex-beauty queen was running an operation in which glamour models were lured into prostitution for clients including politicians and wealthy businessmen, clients from Saudi Arabia and the United Arab Emirates being amongst the best customers.

The girls, some of them less than 18, met clients on locations ranging from 5-star hotels to luxury yachts and charged 10,000 pounds a night.

I often like to say: "Sex if for poor people" with poor tribal people or even teenagers in mind. Prostitution, however, is for people with money to spare, sometimes lots of it.

Myself, I once rented a room briefly to an Italian woman who gave me the phone number of the 'Prostitutes Collective' in St Kilda, Melbourne, asking me to pass on any message for her to that number. I jokingly rang one day and left the message: "There are no messages" and the woman sent the police to tell me that I had violated the telecommunication laws.

The woman once invited me to play billiards with she and a man, I presume her pimp, at St Kilda's famous Esplanade Hotel. I went and the time passed with incident.

Conclusion

I do not think if particularly remarkable or contentious to bracket the fashion, beauty and sex industries as I have here. Indeed, in today's decadent Western societies in particular, we literally enshrine the notion of the beautiful woman as something of a raison d'etre for women and a prime reason for men to be interested in them.

It was not always quite so one-sided, however, and only a few centuries ago well-placed men dressed as extravagantly as women and wore wigs.

What is more remarkable today is men's fashion being based on the business suit and tie, the suit being related in style to army uniforms a century or so ago, and the tie deriving from the cloths Roman soldiers carried ready to bind any sword wound they might suffer.

In other words, men like to both look and act like idiots and do a very good job of it. In contrast women like to look like simple-minded tarts and they do that well too.

On the sex industry Burkina Fasoan President Thomas Sankara made a seemingly religious-based statement:

We should see in every prostitute an accusing finger pointing firmly at society as a whole. Every pimp, every partner in prostitution, turns the knife in this festering and gaping wound that disfigures the world.

Speech at International Women's Day celebration, Quagadougou, March 8, 1987.

Myself, as I say in the Preface of *The Pretentious Persuaders* (2012a), I like to hold that sex was God's joke on mankind. Indeed, with our population at least twice that sustainable with a modern lifestyle, it is perhaps something of a cruel joke now (Mohr, 2012c).

The bottom line, however, is that women are getting on top, an example of this being Heidi Fleiss, experienced in prostitution, planning to open a "stud farm," a brothel for women clients, in the desert town of Crystal, Nevada. In a TV documentary on her plan she said that the availability of Viagra these days makes her plan all the more viable.

Chapter 19

DECAYING WESTERN CIVILIZATION

*Thirty years ago parents were not fighting with their sons and
daughters over piercings and tattoos.
No teeny-bopper heroine sported a stud
through her tongue as Scary Spice does
and sticks her tongue out ostentatiously to prove it.
The tongue stud is supposed to have an erotic function
in stimulating the underside of the penis during fellatio.*
Germaine Greer,
The Whole Woman, Doubleday, London (1999).

Introduction

Western Societies are in deep decay. From advertising of
brothels in free local papers stuffed into every letter box, to
late night TV ads for sex chat, the signs are everywhere to see.
Corruption is everywhere, from priests that molest children to
CEOs with exorbitant salary packages and golden parachutes
when the company sinks. The rat race has become downright
disgusting.

Globalization has made things worse because greedy
companies move manufacturing offshore seeking cheap
labour, forcing their workforces to join the dole queues and
yet still buy their products.

Movies are all too often filled with unbridled violence
topped off with increasingly explicit sex scenes, and half the
population is addicted to either booze, gambling and drugs, if
not all three. Society has become amoral.

The crooks in business

The sheer greed and corruption of 'big biz' grows ever more like the last days of Rome situation, that is, take the money (megabucks) and run. Aristotle held that it was going far enough if the best paid people were remunerated 20 times as much as the worst.

These 'fat cats' now make up to thousands of times more than the slaves who do all the *real work,* that is, producing things we really need, that is, food, clothing and shelter, not just hot air at often booze soaked board meetings..

In recent decades overpaid CEOs have put millions out of work to increase company bottom lines by using cheap overseas labour, and sometimes child labour.

These CEO crooks would be happy to have you send the kids (as well as your partner) to work in the mines once more to pay the rent or mortgage, the latter these days until you are near dead, at which point you can sell the house to get into a nursing home so that you eventually end up with nothing.

The massive profits of the banks in good times are obscene. Businesses need not make huge profits, but the struggling slaves in the work force do need to make enough to save a little for a 'rainy day' in order to avoid being put on the street when they can't afford to pay the rent or mortgage. Again it should be remembered that the Bible holds that one should not profit by lending money. The same sentiment should apply to profiting from what Marx called the 'surplus value' of labour to provide enormous executive salaries (Sweezy, 1946).

Now women too play an increasing role in management and capitalism, as noted by Marxist feminist Evelyn Reed:

Ruling-class women have exactly the same interest in upholding and perpetuating capitalist society as men have. The bourgeois feminists fought, among other things, for the right of women as well as men to hold property in their own name. They won this right. Today, plutocratic women hold fabulous wealth in their own names. They are completely in alliance with the plutocratic men to perpetuate the capitalist system (Reed et al, circa 1970).

The arms industry

That the arms and drug industries are the world's two largest is deplorable. Particularly deplorable are land mines, Agent Orange and depleted uranium munitions which, lamentably, the US used a great deal.

Worse still, a few countries rely on their massive weapons industries to keep afloat economically, no doubt their secret services encouraging wars against the 'commies', countries supposed to harbour terrorists, and disliked heads of state, to help increase sales.

War is expensive, however, and it was just after World War 2 that England's Empire finally collapsed when it surrendered India.

Similarly the USA is now in deep debt, in particular to China, having lost all too many wars, including World War 2 (Stalin won, of course), Korea, Vietnam, Iraq, and Afghanistan.

Indeed, England and the US are now the most indebted countries in history so that now they are both morally and economically bankrupt.

Booze, drugs & gambling

Western societies are now saturated with booze ranging from alcopops for teenagers to all night bars where Greer (1999) laments:

Display of their breasts by topless waitresses earns them better tips; bouncing one's breasts in the face of a complete stranger is a fun way of making a living as a lap-dancer but breast feeding is considered obscene.

An example of how unscrupulous big biz can be is their marketing of cigarettes by giving them out at teenage disco nights. They then soon move on to 'pot' so that in the *Weekend Australian* (2/4/2011) Philip Adams says:

"The 'war on drugs', like so many US wars, is well and truly lost," adding: "We ignore the fact that booze and cigarettes are far, far more destructive to this country than heroin, pot or ecstasy."

In deploring the death and life sentences given to a few Australian "kids" in Bali for smuggling a little pot he concludes: "It would make slightly more sense to save the life sentences for the executives of the cigarette and binge-drinking industries."

The gambling industry is also highly immoral. Seeing people of all ages endlessly pouring money into 'pokies' at all hours in pubs and clubs reminds me strongly of how rats in Skinner boxes demonstrated *operant conditioning* by quickly learning to press a lever in the box to obtain a morsel of food. Before long some of them were manically pressing the lever hundreds of times a minute!

Similarly, we have addicted a whole generation to generally useless Internet browsing and social usage, and PC games to simply lighten their pockets further.

One bloated Australian tycoon was noted for his habit of gambling millions during all night binges in casinos. He got wise eventually, however, and began to buy and build casinos, seeing them as a new and better cash cow than the publishing empire his father had built up.

The sex industry

The burgeoning sex industry is immoral in the extreme, ranging from increasingly ubiquitous brothels and sex shops to a plethora of ridiculous late night ads for phone sex on TV and Internet porn, including child porn which some deviants are insane enough to build up huge collections of on their PC.

Though it should be illegal, there are even ads for brothels in free local newspapers that children of all ages can take out of the letter box before mum and/or dad get home (it is increasingly unlikely that the 'and' applies here).

The media, of course, has got downright dirty, an example being the British reality-TV series Sex Inspectors in which a team of male-female sex therapists installs CCTV cameras in the homes of couples with poor sex lives. Then, with the aid of anatomical diagrams and batteries couples are instructed in masturbation techniques etcetera (Kipnis, 2007).

I don't think things can go much lower than this.

On this point, if not one or two others at least, devout Muslims are not at the extreme and in the wrong, we are!

Mass production with cheap labour

The law of supply and demand is the cornerstone of economics but it applies to agricultural products and commodities so that when the quantity available increases the demand goes down (Wonnacott & Wonnacott, 1979).

For mass produced manufactured goods, however, the production cost per unit decreases as the quantity produced (Q) increases so that, as shown in Fig. 19.1, the 'supply cost' curve goes down.

Then, because of the low price the 'demand' for the product is increased and, as the product gains acceptance the price can be increased gradually.

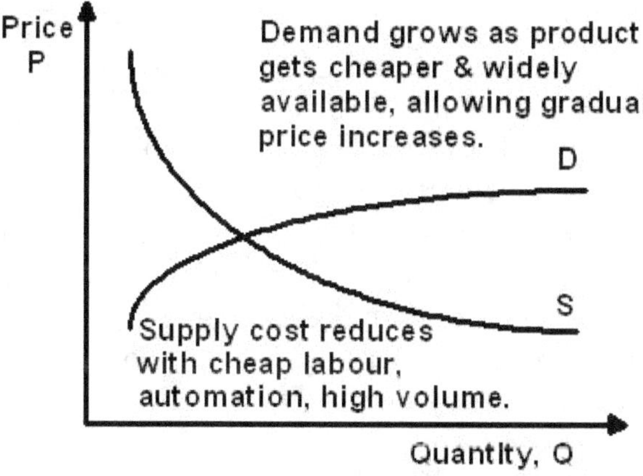

Figure 19.1. Law of supply and demand
for mass produced manufactured products.

Advertising also increases demand, of course, and sadly it is decades of advertising that has enshrined the names of many products now manufactured with cheap labour in Asia.

The problem now is that Asia, and particularly China, have taken over a great deal of manufacturing and in 'The Asian Century' it is they that benefit from Figure 19.1 whilst many Western economies are in crisis.

Declining education standards

Since the 1990s there has been growing discontent amongst many in the education sector in the USA about declining education standards. Their concerns were vindicated by the second international maths study. This found that the top 5% of US students were matched in ability by 50% of Japanese students and the top 1% of US students ranked bottom compared to the top 1% from other countries surveyed.

In algebra and basic calculus Japanese and Chinese students had twice the average score of US students. In geometry the US students ranked in the bottom quarter of the 143 countries surveyed.

Compared with grade eight students from 19 other countries, US students ranked only tenth in arithmetic, twelfth in algebra, and sixteenth in geometry.

A similar, though not as marked, decline in standards has been found in the UK and Australia.

No doubt much of the problem is the increasing immorality and decadence of western societies so that boys are increasingly preoccupied with PC games or ludicrous activities such as spray can graffiti whilst girls are hooked on Facebook and looking like a trendy Barbie Doll.

Declining IQ in the West

Vernon (1960) and Lynn and Vanhaven (2002) point out that we have dysgenic fertility trends so that the least intelligent people have the most children. Burt (1957) found that average IQ in the UK had dropped by 1.5% between the years 1920 and 1950 for this reason and he predicted a further 2.5% drop by the year 2000.

Vernon (1960) also points out that a Royal Commission on Mental Deficiency in the UK discovered a "big increase" in the numbers of defectives between the years 1907 and 1929.

It has also been suggested that IQ in the USA is in decline (Fancher, 1985), some claiming that the rate of decrease is 1 point per generation.

Thus the US ranked a lowly 23 in recent international competency tests of school students (Shanghai came top) and an interviewed US student said her Chinese parents told her that "pupils in China were learning far more advanced concepts."

The implications of declining average intelligence are far reaching. It has been shown, for example, that a drop of just 3 points in average IQ results in increasing numbers of:
(a) Men in jail - 13%.
(b) High school dropouts (permanent) - 15%.
(c) Women chronically dependent on welfare - 15%.

This seems to have come to pass in the USA where, for example, there are more people in jail than attending University.

Once the US produced far more inventions than any other country but, according to a BBC Science report aired on ABC Radio National on 5/4/2011, in 2010 there were 4,000 more foreign applications for US patents then local ones.

Besides the decline in standards of education, another reason for decline in Western intelligence might be our declining moral, ethical and living standards. Another is our increasing predilection for passively watching sport, movies, TV, and only trivial social use of the Internet.

The Westminster system

The Westminster system of government has almost always been a revolving door farce involving two parties taking turns in governing the country for a few years, each switch in government bringing about reversal of many of the changes introduced during the previous period.

Rather than two sides of the parliament engaged in a never-ending and highly comical and witless slanging match, the socialist system of government has a 'ring structure', a central committee with an elected president. In the USSR this often led to massive annual growth rates in GNP but, ultimately, that great 'empire' collapsed circa 1989, as always largely because of the economically debilitating effects of a prolonged war, in this case in Afghanistan.

Now the USSR has a relatively free market economy and a supposedly democratic government, but this is in reality still run by some of the old guard such as Alexander Putin.

China, however, has a seemingly new hybrid form of government, a one-party socialist central committee which governs a relatively free-market economy. Their much more highly controlled economy has the exchange rate pegged to their advantage, much to the displeasure of the sinking USA, resulting in 10% GNP growth rates for well over a decade.

Selling the country

To pay down rising government debt Western governments have been busily selling off public utilities such as electricity, gas and water supply, and telephone and postal services. This, however, is largely a 'one-way street' exercise insofar as it is unlikely that they will ever be able to afford to reverse this privatization process much, if at all.

After such sell-offs there is usually a short honeymoon period when prices and charges are not increased much but, before long the insatiable greed of big biz shows its ugly face and prices rise, often considerably. This is yet another way, then, in which the gap between rich and poor becomes ever wider, now having became a gigantic chasm.

Worse still, having lost most, if not all, their income from cash cow utilities like telecoms, governments are then forced to increases taxes and introduce new ones.

Having already reduced company taxes to lure transnational companies into the country in order to "create jobs," however, the tax changes needed to keep the government debt in check hit the workers, further widening the gap between rich and poor.

In Australia, for example, company tax has almost halved since the 1960s, whereas private income is still taxed at much the same rates. In addition, a GST was introduced in the 1990s and excise on alcohol and cigarettes greatly increased. As in much of the West, house prices have risen far too high, making stamp duty on purchase of a home another major tax on the workers.

Declining living standards in the West

So it is that, whilst bullshitting politicians, journalists, businessmen, economists and other loonies keep raving that we've never had it so good, in reality our real living standards in the West continue to decline.

Now most wives have to work to help pay mortgages on overpriced houses, these mortgages being much overpriced thanks to needlessly excessive interest rates.

Now more and more people are working longer hours, many needing to work two jobs to make ends meet. This is in stark contrast to the standard five day, 40 hour week introduced by law to Australia around a century ago and, indeed, we have not only 7 day operation of most retail businesses but 24/7 operation of many other businesses.

Workplace conditions have become worse in other ways, for example the large open plan offices introduced by the Japanese to allow management to spy on workers every second of the day. Indeed, some companies even have hidden cameras in toilets to make sure people don't spend too long on toilet breaks and their ablutions.

The decline in standards of living for workers reaches absurd proportions for migrant labour living in cupboard-sized rooms annexed to Internet cafes in Japan, or in the case of 6 or more young factory workers from the country living in one room in bunk beds in China.

The bottom line here, indeed, is that many workers have cause for riot and revolution both in the East and West, just as weavers rioted in England at the widespread introduction of powered weaving machines.

The rise and rise of China

The industrial revolution that began in China two or three decades ago, resulting in GDP growth rates circa 10% for the past decade or more, has transformed much of the country. China's economy is now the world's second largest with the USA, although still largest, facing debts from which, like England before it, it may never recover from.

Cheap Chinese products totally dominate the cheap section of the market and 2$+ shops selling cheap household items are now seen scattered throughout the world's cities. No fluke, of course, these are usually run by Chinese people.

Such products exemplify the inverted supply and demand law shown in Figure 19.1, high volume of production along with little or no advertising costs lowering prices enough to stimulate demand.

In the middle price range Chinese goods also take a large share of the market, just one example being LG which has dominated the global market for microwave ovens for over two decades. These are relatively cheap, being a good example of China's low production costs.

With the recent appearance of Great Wall of China cars on the world market China is entering the top price section of the general consumer product market at a time when some other car manufacturers, particularly the US companies, are having trouble surviving.

Other Asian countries are still doing well also, and India is on the rise.

Conclusion

The USA has military and intelligence gathering bases all over the world and is usually involved in military conflict in one or two countries at any one time, either as an active participant or in a logistically supportive role. In Vietnam 3 million civilians were killed, in Iraq one million, and the carnage continues elsewhere now.

All this has come at a cost. California went broke and the US ran budget deficits for many years and its economy was heading for a fall. Toxic loans problems brought some of the country's banks and two of its three major car companies to their knees begging for government bail outs in late 2008, leading to the "Global Financial Crisis" (GFC).

As a result several European countries are in trouble economically, in particular England, Greece, Ireland, Italy, Portugal and Spain, along with some of the former USSR countries.

Like Japan has had since the early 1990s, the US now has had near zero official interest rates since the GFC and in April 2011 a major rating agency put the USA's AAA credit rating "on watch' for two years with a view to a possible downgrade.

The governor of Australia's reserve bank has said that the rise of China was "a transformative event for the global economy," pointing out that China produces almost half the world's steel and 9 times more than the US, and that it has more of the world's top 100 banks (12) than any other country.

He went on to say the integration of China and India into the global economy has "a good way to run yet" and that China would outsize the euro-zone economies within 5 years and approach the US in economic strength terms within a decade (Michael Stutchbury, *The Weekend Australia* April 16-17, 2011).

The bottom line is that, thanks to incompetent government, corrupt capitalism, and social decadence, the last of the great Western empires, that of the USA, has been in decline for decades.

It does seem that this will, indeed, be "The Asian Century", one in which the two most populous nations on earth, China and India will have increasing influence and, before long, China will be the world's largest economy and eventually, perhaps, may take the title of "the world's only superpower" from the USA.

PART 2: SOME SOLUTIONS

Chapter 20

COMPETENT GOVERNMENT

*Economics is as much a study in fantasy and aspirations
as in hard numbers - maybe more so.*
Theodore Roszak, *The Making of a Counter Culture* (1975).

The science [economics] *hangs like a gathering fog in a valley, a fog
which begins nowhere and goes nowhere, an incidental, unmeaning
inconvenience to passers-by.*
H. G. Wells, *A Modern Utopia* (1905).

*If all economists were laid end to end,
they would not reach a conclusion.*
George Bernard Shaw (attributed to).

Introduction

The War of The Sexes has had some good results, for
example delivering equal pay for equal work to many women.
This has coincided with an influx of women into the workforce
after the male workforce was decimated in World War 2.

Since then governments have, as always, been mucking
things up one way or the other. Still wars and terrorism
continued all over the globe, in part stimulated by the arms
industry. Worse still, governments in the West have continually
been pursuing mistaken economic policies, for example
increasing interest rates with the aim of decreasing inflation,
whereas one should usually decrease interest rates to
decrease inflation (Mohr, 2012c).

The result has been cycles of increasing interest rates followed by economic crises causing panicked governments to minimize interest rates again.

In addition, globalization has led to exportation of most jobs in manufacturing to Asia. It has also pressured government into reducing company taxes to attract foreign investment. The result has been increasing government deficits, a situation that has reached crisis point in the USA and some countries in Europe.

With our societies almost in crisis with higher unemployment, 50% divorce rates, and 600,000 children in Australia without a parent that works, concerted action needs to be taken before it is too late.

Real democracy

We need to replace the antiquated and creaking 'revolving door' Westminster system of two parties or coalitions in farcical opposition to one of real democracy.

We need new, more responsible forms of government that don't build up industrial-military states and kowtow to big business but represent *our interests*. All of us should have a *direct* and democratic voice in major decisions at all levels of government and, for that matter, in the running of the organizations that we work for if we are not self-employed.

In other words we should have *freedom*. Specifically, we should have freedom of:

➢ **Speech:** we should be allowed to express our views.

➢ **Opinion:** we should be allowed to democratically express our opinion on *all* major issues.

➢ **Association:** we should be able to meet with and talk to whoever we choose.

➢ **Education:** we should have more educational paths, some of them with faster pacing and shortcuts.

➢ **Careers:** we should have a society in which children develop a vocational idea relatively early in life, rather than a lottery process based on a few marks 'either way' in just one set of exams.

➢ **Employment:** we need a return to the 'a career for life' approach so that people in the workforce are committed to and good at what they do.

➢ **Choice:** industry should provide us with responsible and genuinely innovative and beneficial products which do not have obsolescence built into them.

➢ **Power:** we should have a truly democratic system in which eligible voters are able to vote on all major issues.

The general working public, given real democratic influence, would certainly vote for the proposals of following sections.

Sound economic management

We need sound economic management in which interest rates are not set by ex-bankers with vested interests but set rationally according to sound economic principles such as those of Vernon's LM and IS curves (Vernon 1980).

I give a worked example of these in my recent book *The Doomsday Calculation* (Mohr 2012c) clearly showing that increasing interest rates increases inflation.

In the most advanced economies obsession with economic growth should be reduced. With the world grossly overpopulated and resources fast running out we need to plan for sustainable societies, not growing ones.

Fair wages and taxes

A priority should be to protect local industries and jobs and tariffs are needed for this. In Australia and elsewhere tariffs have been almost totally eliminated and industry has been decimated as a result. Tariffs on car imports, for example are now only about 5%, whereas they are more like 15% in China.

Obscenely bloated executive salary packages should be prevented by setting sensible limits on remuneration. This would increase the minimum wage by at least 5%, a good start.

Profit proportional company taxes should be introduced (last I heard this is the case in the USA). The range for these should be 50% for anything like substantial profits, rising to circa 75% for high profit levels.

Personal income tax should be reduced for low income earners and increased for high income earners, with the top rate being perhaps 75%.

The justification for these taxation changes is simply that people or companies with high earnings are making more than their fair share out of the money circulating in the community at large.

This can be illustrated by the classical equation of exchange of the monetarist economic theory:

$$MV = PQ.$$

where V = the *velocity of money*, M = the quantity of money in public hands, P = average level of prices, Q = quantity of output.

Here V = the number of times M is spent to buy Q during the year and my point is that if some greedy people manage to 'trap' more of the money in circulation then, as it is a 'general' pool of money, they took more than their fair 'share' and should return some of it via taxes.

Buy back the country

Government should buy back essential utilities such as electricity, gas and water supplies. These were once cash cows for governments and provided a substantial proportion of their income. Carving them into nominal pieces, such that numerous separate organizations collect customer payments, has resulted in farcical wastage of money through duplication of resources and competitive marketing.

Government should also own at least two of the four or five largest commercial banks to provide control in the sector where now profits are obscene in good times whilst in bad times some banks have to be bailed out at great public expense, a farcical situation.

Statutory reserve deposits for banks were once circa 10% but have now sunk to more like 2% in many counties, a precarious situation in part responsible for the European Financial Crisis of 2010+.

Democratic Management

Rather than shift the 'real work' overseas, it might be better to sack the entire management and leave their task to the workers who would certainly be prepared to take half a day a week off to attend management meetings. At these, 'MBA in a book' publications could be handed out, and this would probably achieve better results than hiring Harvard and the like MBA graduates.

That way, for example, Human Resource departments, a nasty term that originated in Harvard, could be done away with, and recruitment could be dealt with by the 'workers management committee' whilst financial matters, including those of remuneration, could be dealt with by an accountant or two in all but the largest of organizations.

Concerning equity finance for companies, an original and interesting proposal was made by Peter Jay (1981), a former economics editor of London's *The Times* newspaper:

– that the enterprises which create the wealth, the firms, the corporations, should belong to, be owned by, should have their directors exclusively appointed by and their net assets and their residual earnings should belong to, and exclusively to, the people who work at them.

Jay suggested that it is an accident of history, not a law of economics, that the entrepreneur has tended to be the person who supplied the risk capital. He proposed that in modern economies worker-owned companies should be able to raise debt finance from banks and equity finance from shareholders in the usual way.

Capitalists are happy to have their workers become shareholders, of course, because shareholders do not have to be paid dividends in bad times, whereas banks always require interest to be paid on loans.

Jay's proposal goes a lot further and might eliminate the absurd salaries, share and rights bonuses, and retirement packages for CEOs we see today. Indeed, it would only seem fair that *all* workers for a corporation should receive share issues as a non-taxable part of their income.

Supporting family life

In many countries in the West real living standards have fallen in recent decades, despite the usual bullshit from high in the hierarchy that we've never had it so good.

For many people working hours have increased well beyond the 40 hours decided upon as a sensible norm almost a hundred years ago in Australia.

With the world overpopulated to the point that it is impossible to provide jobs for all, it would be sensible to make a 4 day week standard. This could be made up of 9 hour days, giving a total of 36 hours per week, only a 10% reduction. The change in lifestyle would be enormous, cutting commuting congestion, times and costs, and even stimulating consumer spending via the extra day off.

Then, in intact families where both husband and wife work full-time, they would only work a total of 8 days and could have 2 extra days a week when one parent was at home to deal with family and household matters, a considerable improvement in lifestyle.

In addition, there should be government support at some modest level to encourage women, and sometimes husbands perhaps, to stay at home to look after children and homes.

Given a 4 day week was standard it could become a sensible norm for housewives to take a part-time job for one or two days a week to supplement family income, still leaving at least one day with the whole family at home.

Education

As noted in that last chapter, education standards and IQ are decreasing in much of the decadent West.

Not only do we need to rid our society of drugs and reduce the antisocial booze, gambling, and sex industries, but we also need to teach children more about real life at school rather than simply spin out the Three Rs and little more over year after boring year.

Children should be helped and counseled to develop a realistic career 'area' early in life and then helped to achieve it.

There should also be courses in 'life management' dealing with such issues as bullying and consumerism so that they do not get into trouble in such areas.

In addition, they should be taught about how to plan their personal lives, emphasizing that the world is already greatly overpopulated and that they should be very careful to avoid unplanned pregnancies. Indeed, it should be emphasized that the act of sex is merely one of procreation and, rather than being viewed as fun, should be taken very seriously indeed, and then only in the context of a relatively long-term relationship and, preferably, a marriage.

Conclusion

Only a few examples are given here, but clearly a great deal can and should be done to improve national economic and living standards.

Chapter 21

FINDING A PARTNER

Wisest men
Have erred, and by bad women been deceived;
And shall again, pretend they ne'er so wise.
John Milton, *Samson Agonistes* 1, 210 (1671).

While this is one of the most famous of Old Testament
pairings, a first-degree fatal attraction that is also the first of
its kind, the first episode of the femme fatale – of a woman
whose mere existence is a contagious airborne virus
for that certain susceptible sucker of a man.
Elizabeth Wurtzel, *Bitch, In Praise of Difficult Women* (1998).

Introduction

In the old days boys meeting girls with a view to learning about the opposite sex was harder to do, especially if one went to a single sex school. Then dances run for teenagers were just about the only formal opportunity for 'research' so that it was not highly uncommon for a man to end up marrying a girl from the same or a nearby school, or who lived in the same street, or who even lived next door.

These days there are youth centres for school-age children to meet up to five days a week and also at regular special functions.

Once one reaches 18 there are pubs and clubs, of course, and even Internet and phone services advertised on late-night TV that introduce lonely people.

Today, of course, younger people often share flats and houses and, of course, that is a way of meeting the opposite sex. Indeed, it is my experience more than once that advertising a room in a house is a quite likely way of finding a friend and women know this full well. They are fully aware of the possible consequences of living in the same abode as another man and, indeed, often seek to meet a man in this way.

Love at first sight?

When a single person looking for a partner meets a person of the opposite sex they should try to form a sound opinion of the person by considering such factors as:
- Looks.
- Body language. This is especially important including how does it feel to have the person close to you?
- Personality.
- Do they seem relaxed or nervous meeting you?
- Do they seem genuinely pleased to meet you?
- Their age, occupation and educational background.
- Have they been single for long? If so, why?
- Where did their parents come from?
- What do her parents do?

This is quite a lot of data to gather and it may take more than one meeting to acquire it. At the first meeting a kiss or hug or two is OK but nothing more than that should be considered. If either person is too drunk to care about this limitation then that should end the first meeting. If polite refusal causes offence that is good reason to end the first meeting and never have another one.

If a second meeting is had that allows time to complete the foregoing data list and assess the person and also assess your own feelings for the person. The second meeting, however, is still too soon to sensibly consider having sex with the person.

Further research

On meeting the new person for the second and subsequent times it may be useful to consider how both they and you rate in terms of the 'CAB' response illustrated in Figure 21.1.

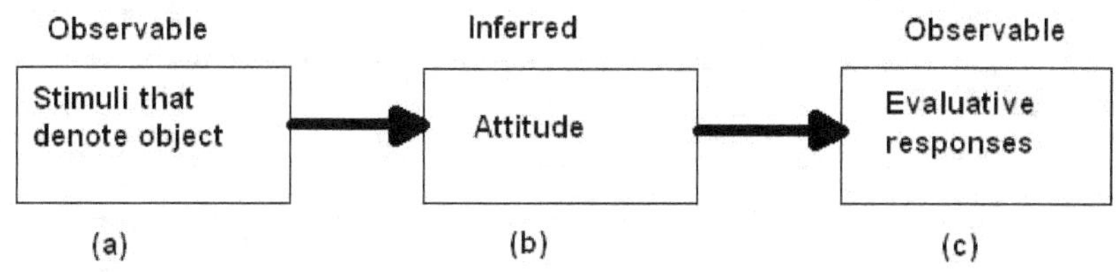

Figure 21.1. Cognitive, attitudinal, and behavioral responses.

Here Figure 21.1 illustrates the three types of response involved in attitudinal psychology (Eagly & Chaiken, 1993). These are:

1. *Cognitive response* or recognition of a stimulus, in this case seeing the person again.
2. *Affective response* or the feelings or emotions this recognition gives you..
3. *Behavioural response* or what you think you would now like to do.

Evaluating your response to the a new acquaintance is important, as is estimating what you think their response to you is. In both cases the cognitive response should be instant recognition, followed by facial expressions and body language that indicate attitude, and finally behaviour such as, for example, turning away from you which, of course, is probably a sure sign of negative feelings.

If things go so far as meeting two or three times you should be in a position to make a decision table to evaluate the new friend and thus decide whether to continue the relationship for a significant period.

Table 21.1. Decision table.

	Scores/10	
Attribute	**Person A**	**Person B**
Looks		
Body language		
Personality		
Talkative		
Apparent IQ		
Family background		
Education		
Occupation		
Honesty (perceived)		
Good worker?		
Generous		
Friends or a loner?		
Sex OK		
TOTAL		

Table 21.1 is a decision table comparing the attributes of two people using Likert Scaling (Likert 1961; Eagly & Chaiken 1993). Obviously if one has a much better score than the other then that might suggest them as a better partner for a long-term relationship.

Believe it or not, a woman I once met when divorced put me under a tiny bit of pressure on the commitment issue and I responded by suggesting such a table. She duly compiled one and in the column for me the score for sex was blanked out, perhaps mercifully!

On a more serious note, communication depends in part sometimes in what two people have in common to talk about, for example, what to have for dinner, or their children. At the beginning of a relationship, however, it is far more important to assess whether there is much in your respective personal and family backgrounds to talk about.

Do you for example, have similar tastes in music, literature and sport? Are you both the 'arty' or the scientific types? And so on, but very important.

Communication will also depend, in part at least, on intelligence. When you talk about a certain subject does the other person sometimes quickly respond with new information or a useful suggestion? If so, that is a sign of intelligence.

Jencks et al. (1975) report that men with IQs of 120 have wives with an average IQ of 111 and that wives with an IQ of 120 have husbands with an average IQ of 111.

Thus they have not married randomly for, had they done so, their partners would have an average IQ of 100.

Living together

The decision whether or not to live together should be based on data such as that required for Table 21.1 and, of course, should not be made in haste.

Only a few decades ago unmarried men and women living together were deemed to be living in sin and whether or not to get married usually took years to decide.

This has changed greatly but still the decision on whether to live in a de facto marriage situation should not be taken lightly and only after the relationship has lasted at least a few months without problems:

I have only ever refused to marry one couple,
and that was because they had only just met.
The whole thing sounded good in theory. There simply hadn't
been enough time for the process of deliberation.
I told them that if they wanted to get married, they could go to
a registry office and in a month's time they would be husband
and wife but, If they wanted me to do the ceremony, come
back and see me in four or five months and we would see how
they were getting on.
Within a couple of weeks their relationship was over.
Philip Baker, *Decisions of Daring Achievers* (2004).

When a couple do decide to live together that is only a beginning of sorts. Presumably sex has been tried out a good deal before cohabiting, hopefully with effective contraceptive measures in place. Such measures should continue, of course, until the relationship has lasted for, preferably, a few years.

At that point the relationship can be carefully reassessed and a decision made as to whether it should be continued, perhaps with the help of opinions and advice from friends and relatives.

If so, the question of children might be considered, but only after careful thought and planning, including careful consideration of whether the job and financial prospects of one, if not both, partners are secure for the long term.

On the important question of children advice is essential from friends, relatives and preferably a professional counselor, the bottom line being that marriage and relationship guidance counselors are needed before marriage, and most certainly before having children, not when the marriage strikes problems.

Indeed, independent advisors can consider the physical, emotional, and financial conditions of the relationship and thus take a 'potential child's' point of view in deciding whether it should be had.

Similarly, I would urge couples with children considering breaking up to be more democratic and consider their children's view of the matter also.

Chapter 22

FAMILY PLANNING

Half of all pregnancies in Britain are unplanned.
One in five will end in termination.
Statement issued by the alliance of FPA, BCT,
Brook Advisory Centres and the Health Education Authority,
1988, quoted in *The Whole Woman,* Greer (1999).

Introduction

All too often, even before a couple has decided to live together, pregnancy occurs and this may force the issue. This is an unfortunate situation that should be avoided at all costs because it puts great pressure on the relationship from the beginning. Instead of the couple getting to know each other and building a secure relationship and financial situation over a period of a few years, those early years are dominated by the unexpected demands and expenses of a child.

In the old days this situation was often the beginning of a lifelong poverty trap and these days it is often likely to result in the couple separating after a few years, a tragic result for all concerned, especially children.

Research has found that, as might be expected, children given more resources and attention, especially from the outset, do better at school and in later life.

Thus would-be parents owe it to their children to plan for them as well as possible.

Planning to have children

Considerable thought should be given to choosing a partner for a long-term relationship. Then the decision as to whether to live together (and get married at that point or later) should only be taken on the basis of advice from friends and relatives, and then only after the relationship has lasted at least a few months, preferably a year or two.

Living together already suggests the possibility of children, but that step should only be considered when the relationship is financially and emotionally secure, and on the basis of further advice and perhaps professional counseling.

Planning for the first child should include consideration of whether one's home is suitable for a child, whether at least one of the parents-to-be has a secure career, and whether the relationship is happy, stable and likely to be permanent.

Financial security is very important too, of course, and one should not consider having children unless one is in a secure financial position. Preferably, for example, one would already have bought one's own apartment or house and be able to manage the mortgage repayments of that as well as the increased living expenses that a child will bring.

The appearance of 'the pill' in the 1960s has, of course, made the task of family planning a great deal easier and Caro and Fox (2008) feel that the pill and tampon freed women considerably.

In addition, we now have the 'morning after' pill and the pill for men is in the research and development pipeline.

How many children?

The question of how many children a couple should have is, of course, a very important one.

In Victorian times in England families had between five and seven children but by the 1960s this had declined to just over two (Worsley, 1970). Indeed, circa 1960 my father said he believed in "ZPG" (zero population growth) and thence 2-child families, and the world would now be a much better place if that had, indeed, happened.

Less than a century ago large families were still common but now, in an overpopulated world with real living standards decreasing in the West, that is not an option for most people. Ordinary working people simply cannot afford it and rich people are usually careful not to have too many children and thus 'dilute' the family wealth.

China had an effective one child policy in place for a few decades and, indeed, only children are usually more intelligent, in part, of course, because they receive more care and attention (Vernon, 1960).

Weiss and Mann (1978), for example, refer to a project in Milwaukee that found that children given more attention by the mother or a specially trained teacher, showed markedly higher IQ.

Two children is, of course, a sensible number for those that can afford it. Both should be able to receive sufficient attention and resources to ensure a good upbringing.

A female relative of mine had a son, and then a second son not long after. Wanting a girl, I suspect with some urging from her own mother, she had a third child which was a girl. Indeed, she had taken some strange but doubtful measures to make having a girl more likely.

Then, hoping to balance the numbers, she had a fourth and last child but that turned out to be a boy. In the end four children in about 6 years really proved too much for them to deal with in terms of attention and discipline and two of the four children had serious problems with drugs, one of them ending up a hopeless schizophrenic mess.

Myself, having had two children and been divorced, I was fortunate to escape one marriage when the woman had a miscarriage. I escaped a second time when a woman became pregnant but was told the child would be "mildly retarded." Consulting experts I found that this really meant quite severe retardation and this information persuaded the woman to have an abortion at five months, perhaps a good example of how important it is to get advice sometimes.

Working mothers

If a family has only one or two children the mother, especially if she has a professional career for which she did years of training, may want to return to the workforce when at least one of the children are still young.

This will require the use of a day care centre and this is quite expensive, costing around $100 per day at present in Australia.

This cost usually comes out of post-tax earnings so that the cost of having two children in day care can easily erode most of a woman's wages, some women reporting that they earn as little as $50 a week after childcare is deducted.

At this point, of course, many women opt out of the workforce and become housewives.

As Bryson (1992) points out, from a social point of view, indeed, a woman staying at home caring for her children is making her contribution:

Marx and Engels did say that reproduction as well as production was a part of the material basis of society. In the 'German Ideology' they wrote of "the production of life, both of one's own in labour and of fresh life in procreation."

In addition, stay at home mothers may be in a better position to give their children a head start in learning, a matter discussed further in Chapter 24.

Conclusion

A couple should only consider having children after their relationship has lasted a substantial time, preferably a few years. Then whether or not to have children should be decided on the basis of advice from friends, relatives and perhaps professional counselors.

Then, of course, the couple should make sure that their home is suitable for children and that their finances are sufficient and secure for the long term.

Finally, they should try to imagine whether a child would want to live in their home with them, or would it prefer other, better circumstances.

Most important of all, the relationship should be a permanent one because parents are the most important influence in a child's life.

As Morgan et al. (1979) put it:

For many reasons, the family is the prime site for observational learning during childhood. Parents are children's first models as well as their first teachers. They are also very powerful figures in young children's lives, controlling all resources and caring for all needs. Children watch their parents do many things which look like fun, and see that many skills their parents have are effective (lead to better reinforcement) than their own skills.

Thus to give children a good start in life a stable, adequately financed and happy marriage is required.

Then both parents should stick at the task of keeping family life happy and secure and make a considerable effort at teaching and bringing up their children as best they can.

Chapter 23

MAKING MARRIAGE WORK

*To be required to sleep with the same woman forever was a
curious and unnatural idea to him, to be expected to dredge
up enthusiasm for old acts, and routine plays,
he wondered at the arrogance of the female.*
Tom Morrison, *The Bluest Eye* (1970).

*I did not sleep. I never do when I am over-happy,
under-happy, or in bed with a strange man.*
Edna O'Brien, *The Love Object* (1968).

Mohr's Law of Politics

Making marriage, or an equivalent relationship, work is
less than easy. Mohr's Law of Politics is that build a 'fence' of
any kind and there will be people in substantial numbers on
either side of it as potential competitors (Mohr, 2018b).

Some political divisions are comparatively arbitrary
compared to the considerable differences between men and
women, some of which were discussed in earlier chapters of
this book.

Women's ability to bear children is a very major difference,
one that men are somewhat in awe of. Women, on the other
hand, are sometimes in awe of men's greater strength and,
indeed, sometimes in fear of it. The latter difference we
evolved with and it was the basis of our survival in our
troglodyte hunter-gathering days.

As noted in Chapter 21 there are many other differences between two marriage partners. As Baker (2004) points out:

Gender aside, the potential for conflicts continues to abound. We come from difference places and are affected more than we understand by our family of origin.

Then, for example only, there are differences in personality, habitual behavioural differences, differences in educational and work background, and differences in likes and dislikes.

Communication

Lack of effective and constructive communication is the great problem of the human race. What makes us unique amongst animals is our enlarged cerebral cortex that stores the semantic memory required for our advanced languages.

Yet throughout history we have continued to behave just like the chimps that Jane Goodall (van Lawick-Goodall, 1971) was so disillusioned by, we have periodic conflicts with other groups of people, be it tribes, nations or followers of another religion.

This is largely because of a lack of *effective* communication and thence *understanding* of other people.

Such understanding is, of course, made more difficult when people speak a different language, but men and women also, in effect, speak different languages to some extent at least, in part because of their different upbringing, and thence different issues and related vocabulary, as discussed in Chapter 7.

As a result of their different, somewhat socially stereotyped, upbringing, men and women have different values. Women, of course, care more about children, in part owing to the powerful maternal instinct discussed in Chapter 6. Men, on the other hand, care more about the football team they follow winning, and such comparatively trivial pursuits tend to alienate them from many women.

There are many more minor differences. Women care much more about their appearance, having been brought up supposed to look beautiful. Men's business suits, on the other hand, relate to army uniforms and are designed to make them look stupid, not hard to do.

These differences, of course, make communication difficult. As a somewhat tongue-in-cheek test of this, try sending a member of an all-male board to a meeting dressed as a woman!

In a marital-type relationship, however, I would recommend that the partners have some sort of discussion every day or two. At this they can air their respective gripes about each other, if any, and it is far better to bring them out in the open in this way than risk the other partner complaining to other people about you as this may result in rumours which may be damaging to your reputation.

Perhaps more important, the partners should discuss any problems they may be having at work as these may pose a risk to a partner's career. Problems with their children should, of course, also be discussed.

Finally, financial matters should be discussed occasionally to make sure that the family financial situation is sound.

Partnership

A marital-type relationship should, of course, be a partnership and the work should be shared. In the traditional male breadwinner scenario housewives would always complain that they were still busy cooking and dealing with children after the man had finished work, giving rise to the old saying: "A woman's work is never done."

Today, a high proportion of wives are also employed at least part-time, as noted in Chapter 22, often requiring expensive day care for children, and this places a considerable financial stress on many families that are also struggling to pay substantial rents or mortgages.

Even when both partners work full-time, however, most women find themselves doing most of the housework, leading to continuing complaints:

Women still do around 80 per cent of home chores and caring tasks, despite their increased workforce participation. Helene Couprie, Time Allocation within the Family, *Economic Journal,* 2007.

It found single working women spent an average of ten hours a week doing housework and single men seven hours. After becoming a couple, women's housework time shot up to 15 hours a week, while the average male contribution dropped to five hours, even when both spouses work outside the home (Caro & Fox, 2008).

The problem relates to the traditional housewife role of women, of course, and the solution is that men should be encouraged to spend more time helping with both housework and caring for and teaching children.

If the working woman cum housewife then has a little more spare time that can be spent relaxing and talking with their partner, thus helping keep the relationship working congenially and effectively.

Healthy life

Healthy lifestyle should be a primary objective in every family, this including sound diet, watching one's weight, getting enough exercise, getting plenty of quality sleep, and getting enough relaxation time.

A healthy diet should, of course, include plenty of vegetables and a little fruit, limit fat (particularly saturated and trans fat) and thence meat (especially red meat), limit fatty fast food, limit fatty and salty snack foods, and limit sugary confectionary and drinks.

Children should limit sugar, of course, to protect their teeth, also brushing them soon after eating. Indeed, I find it lamentable that there is no provision for this at school.

Watching one's weight and exercise, of course, go together, and it is important to keep one's weight fairly close to that recommended for one's height and sex (Mohr, 2012b, 2013, 2015, 2018c).

To help build strong bodies children should have about an hour of exercise daily, including walking, and when old enough they should be encouraged to do an average of half an hour of more strenuous exercise daily.

For good health the same exercise requirements apply to adults, regular medium intensity exercise being required for a healthy heart and circulation system, for example.

A few hours of relaxation time is also necessary and this, of course, can include such entertainments as TV, music and reading.

For adults circa 8 hours of good quality sleep is necessary for good mental and physical health. Here the shared double bed can be a problem. If, for example, one partner snores, as is often the case, that can pose serious problems. Lonely young children invading the room in the middle of the night is another problem lessened (roughly halved, in fact) if the parents have separate rooms.

Sexual intercourse is merely an act of breeding which humans, being in most respects the most stupid creatures on the planet, as our always troubled history suggests, attach much too much importance to. As I like to say, sex was God's joke on mankind and we are too stupid to see it.

On the issue of satisfactory sex, according to the landmark Kinsey report, 10 percent of married women had never had orgasm during sexual intercourse, and 25 percent had not had orgasm during the first year of marriage (Lindzey et al, 1978).

I think that a couple's sex life might be better if they slept in separate beds, if not separate rooms, especially if one partner snores. Then, refreshed by sleeping well each night, a little 'mucking around' could be done on a more occasional basis if both partners had a double bed, even if in separate rooms, but perhaps with a shared bathroom between them.

The bottom line is that sharing a bed for life with the same ultimately rotting thing is arguably insane, and certainly physically unhealthy, if not distasteful, if one had half one's wits left that is.

Conclusion

One problem in marriage is that, as noted in Chapters 2 and 3, young men are not brought up thinking about children and romance. Often they are really just finding their way in the world a little when they have their first sexual relationship or two with women. When they all too often end up with unplanned for children they are completely unprepared for the situation.

Young women, on the other hand, have been brought up playing with dolls, and for them children are a raison d'etre. In addition, they see getting married to some nice man and having children as being romantic. Indeed, much of the huge publishing and movie industries are based on this.

Thus, when the somewhat humdrum reality of marriage with wailing children emerges women are often quite disillusioned.

No doubt that is why we call that holiday taken after marriage the honeymoon, because reality will hit when the honeymoon ends, of course.

For marriage to work the relationship must have been a carefully chosen one in the beginning, as discussed in Chapter 21. Then the marriage should only have been made after careful thought and advice, and after the relationship has endured for a substantial amount of time.

More important still, children should only be had if the relationship is likely to last, and after plenty of thought, discussion, advice and counseling, along with proper career and financial planning.

Then, to keep the partnership working well, frequent and effective communication and planning is required, along with optimism or 'hope' (GA, RS & PE Mohr., 2018b), to ensure a healthy and happy life for the whole family.

Chapter 24

MAKING YOUR CHILDREN SMARTER

In the present writer's survey of Army recruits (Vernon, 1951), for example, the average I.Q. of those who were only children, or who had but one sibling, was about 106; but with each additional child sibling the figure declined till those from families of 13 and over averaged only 87.
Philip Vernon, *Intelligence and Attainment Tests* (1960).

Introduction

As noted in the quotation above, having only one or two children makes them more likely to have a higher IQ, doubtless because of the greater resources and attention able to be given to the children.

Indeed, China's one child policy of the last couple of decades may be further proof of this because average intelligence in that part of Asia is now, at circa 100.25, slightly above that for the UK and USA (supposedly about 100, but I suspect somewhat less [Mohr, 2012a; Mohr & Fear, 2016; Mohr et al., 2018a]).

Man's population is also at least double what is sustainable with any degree of comfort (Mohr, 2012c), so having only one or two children is the only sensible course on that score.

As noted in earlier chapters, care should always be taken in family planning, waiting until financial and emotional stability of the relationship is assured before having children.

It should also be noted that, as Lynn and Vanhaven (2002) point out, we have dysgenic fertility trends so that the least intelligent people have the most children.

Carlo Cipolla (1974) pointed out that our population growth graph went almost vertical with the coming of the industrial revolution and implored that what we needed was 'quality not quantity,' a phrase I recall my fifth grade teacher Miss Bachelard repeating often.

As noted in earlier chapters, in seeking a compatible partner intelligence is a key criterion. Then couples with higher intelligence might expect at least equally intelligent children, the desirable outcome.

Couples should also be aware of epigenic marking before having children because traits such as obesity are passed on in that way. Thus it is also possible that traits such as exercising or thinking a lot might be passed on also.

Early brain development

At birth the human brain is relatively large compared to the body. Almost all the neural cells that will ever be available are present but only a basic network of the *axons* and *dendrites* that connect *neurons* together exists. Further connections develop as the infant learns basic perception and motor skills, the long *axons* that extend from the brain cells then receiving signals from *receptor cells,* such as the small hair cells in the inner ear, or sending signals to *effector cells* in the muscles.

This development in the bulk of the brain parallels that in all animal species and is that necessary for basic functioning and survival. What sets humans apart is the considerable development of the *cerebral cortex*, the envelope of brain cells that covers the brain, and where our thinking and storage of abstract memory information such as language occurs.

Development of the articulatory mechanisms required for controlled speech and the cortical mechanisms that control them is a slow maturational process that occurs in *Broca's area* of the frontal cortex. It has been suggested that babbling, however, is a sub cortical process.

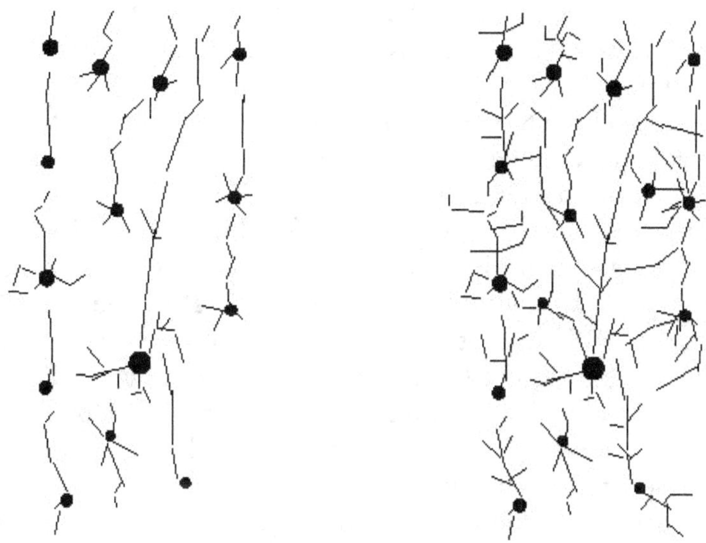

Figure 24.1. Postnatal development of the human cerebral cortex around Broca's Area (language related):
(a) newborn; (b) 1 month.

Semantic memory of language is stored in *Wernicke's area* of the temporal lobe of the cerebral cortex.

Figure 24.1(a) shows a small part of the cerebral cortex of a newborn child in which long *axons* extend from the neurons and form branches. Fine *terminal arbors* at the end of these branches connect at *synapses* to the short *dendrites* surrounding other neurons. Figure 24.1(b) shows considerably more dendrites and branching of the axons at the age of one month (Foss & Hakes, 1978). At the age of 24 months the neural network is a good deal denser.

At birth every neuron can connect with 2,500 other neurons. At age 2 or 3 there are 2 billion neurons and each can connect to up to 15,000 other neurons (Holford, 2008). The network continues to develop in following years and the neurons, while not increasing in number, do increase in size.

In addition, the motor nerve pathways that control such activities as speech production must gradually develop sheaths of the protein *myelin* that prevent 'short-circuiting' of impulses between nerve tracts.

As a result of this gradual brain development each human characteristic is developed at a different rate.

Eye coordination, for example, develops much more rapidly than speech. Nevertheless, for the first few months the infant may smile at any moving object such as a dummy head whereas later it may be upset by the faces of strangers.

Packard (1978) cites a vivid example of the importance of timing. In this two Harvard researchers studied the way kittens learnt to recognize shapes and patterns, a physiological ability that develops in the fourth week. If the kittens were blindfolded for this week they effectively became blind for life. There appear, therefore, to be periods when the infant's brain is extraordinarily receptive to behavioural and personality development so that it is easiest to change a child's intelligence for better or worse before the age of four.

Vocabulary growth in early childhood

When children reach the age of one the pace at which learning can take place greatly increases.

Now learning can be accomplished with a host of aids such as pictures, simple books and educational toys.

By this formative age the child has been out and about a good deal and optimistic attempts have been made to teach it many words of which it will have learnt only a few.

As shown in Table 24.1, however, word learning occurs at a quite rapid rate from here on, to the point at which a basic command of language has been obtained at age five.

Table 24.1. Words learnt with age.

Age (years)	Words learnt
1	3-5
1.25	15
1.5	25
1.75	100
2	250
2.5	450
3	900
4	1550
4.5	1900
5	2100
5.5	2300
6	2550

Whilst the first year is instrumental in learning to begin to talk, in the second year a comparatively massive growth in vocabulary occurs. Thereafter the rate of increase is approximately linear but slows down as the child comes to grip with a widening range of subjects at school.

Note that care should be taken to teach children numbers amongst their earliest words, and to teach them to make simple sums such as 2 + 2 = 4.

By the time they have learnt to read a little, however, children are able to learn things by *cognitive* learning which *processes* and stores *abstract* information.

At this stage they can be taught concepts such as good and bad, and this is in turn helpful in motivating their learning progress.

Finally, one should aim for a child being at least a little ahead of the results of Table 24.1, and having comparable performance in numeracy to that of Table 24.1.

The early learning centre

At the outset an infant's cot and simple learning objects that might be placed in view of it are the child's first learning centre. When a child is about one year old this learning centre might be upgraded to a small child's table plus simple books and other educational aids and toys.

The importance of this *enrichment* of the child's learning environment was tellingly demonstrated by the work of social psychologist David Krech and his group at UC Berkeley (Packard, 1978).

In this they provided a group of rats with an "enriched environment" of large cages with various things rats enjoy such as slides, wheels and the like. Then a maze with a sugar reward at the end was added. This had a dark and a lighted alley and the rats soon learnt which led to the sugar. Then the maze lighting was reversed regularly so that the rats had to relearn the 'sugar route.'

A second control group of rats lived normally and a third group was kept in a deprived dark and noiseless area.

After 90 days it was found that the 'enriched' rats had developed thicker cerebral cortexes!

This was perhaps the first evidence that the brain is modified by experience. The enrichment conditions caused the following changes (Atrens & Curthoys, 1982):

[1] The size of the cerebral cortex was increased.
[2] The size of the cortical neurons increased.
[3] The size and number of synaptic contacts increased.
[4] The quantity of acetylcholinesterase, the compound responsible for breakdown of the neurotransmitter acetylcholine, increased.

Therefore, the rats which had experienced early environmental enrichment were apparently anatomically and biochemically superior to those which had endured a deprived environment.

This result provided laboratory evidence that environmental enrichment might be able to reverse the deficiencies in brain development resulting from an environmentally deprived childhood.

The conclusion, of course, is that, just as physical exercise is good for your body, mental exercise helps develop the brain, perhaps in synergy with an enriched physical environment that includes physical activities involving some intelligence and skill.

Maria Montessori provided evidence that an enriched environment accelerates human learning ability by taking poor children in Rome and placing them in stimulating classrooms with many interesting puzzles and objects to work with. The children were reading enthusiastically by three or four and were well into geometry by five or six.

If follows that the investment of a modest amount of money in setting up and equipping a child's personal learning centre might be a wise one.

Increasingly the child will have learnt to spend time in this engaged in learning activities such as looking at picture books, drawing, learning to write, and so on.

Parents should also have made a point of not only supervising this important activity at least intermittently but also joining in for a substantial session of one-on-one instruction.

By now the child is capable of discussing its problems and progress and asking questions that might help solve problems and assist progress. Therefore, the parent should make a point of allowing a time period of at least several minutes every few days in which to talk with the child in this way.

The importance of the home environment was emphasized in a study by Bradley and Caldwell (1967) in which an inventory of favourable factors in the home was compared to the results from a test of the infant's development:

A group of 77 normal children was given an infant development test and a home assessment inventory at age 6 months, and the Stanford-Binet at age 3 years.

*It was found that the home inventory
predicted IQ at age 3 better than did
the infants' own mental development at 6 months!
Children with increasing scores had mothers who were
involved with them and provided appropriate play materials;
those with decreasing scores tended to live in homes
where material things and daily events were disorganized.*

Much of the correlation between home environment and IQ development can be ascribed to heredity but a study by Skodal and Skeels (1949) showed that improved environment increased children's IQs by an average of 20 points above that of their mothers.

Two heads are better than one

It is, of course, better when both parents take an active part in a child's home learning. Having two teachers 'on the same page' about everything taught will, of course, reinforce the child's learning efforts.

In addition, variation from a woman's softer touch to a man's perhaps more goal-oriented approach can help with progression through longer learning tasks.

It has been found that correlation of intelligence with parent's occupation is slightly less than that for genes (Vernon, 1960), there being, of course, a correlation between occupations and intelligence in any case.

More important, regardless of a parent's occupation, if one of their roles is active teaching of the child that may have a far more important bearing on the child's IQ development than the parent's occupation outside the home.

A sound routine for home learning should be established, perhaps involving a combination of day care or learning groups (as discussed in the next section) and home sessions once or twice a day and of duration ranging from half an hour to an hour, depending on the child's age.

Small learning groups

Packard (1978) raised the interesting possibility of the use of professional people to teach by modeling.

These people would be trained to know the periods during which learning of various areas of knowledge can best be commenced, and in how best to use modeling techniques to initiate that learning. Such people would then visit the home or attend play group sessions.

Packard noted that an experiment with a form of group modeling was undertaken at New York Medical College. This began with twenty pairs of mothers and babies when the babies were only four weeks old and lasted three years at the end of which the children were compared with those of a control group.

The children in the experimental group were a good deal more advanced in language and other skills than the control group.

Indeed, some experts doubt the competence of the modern family for child rearing and believe that more professional efforts are essential to help develop emotional stability and intellectual development in infants.

As an example of this, Weiss and Mann (1978) refer to a project in Milwaukee that found that children given more attention by the mother or a specially trained teacher, showed markedly higher IQ.

Enhancing the learning process

The home learning process can be enhanced by such means as the 'Superlearning' recommended by Ostrander and Schroeder (1979). This involves encouraging physical and psychological relaxation with quite background music, slow breathing exercises, and visualizing nice scenes to achieve a reflective and receptive frame of mind.

Then the child is encouraged to affirm: "I can do it."

Here, developing a positive attitude is comparable to the 'teacher expectancy effect' where it is found that students who already get good marks are encouraged to do even better by a combination of the positive results, the confidence they obtain from these, and the 'expectation' and confidence the teacher shows about their ability.

With the scene set, the parent/teacher reads the material aloud at a careful pace while the child reads it silently. This is repeated again with quiet background music and the child is then tested on the material.

Home schooling

In the USA home schooling has increased markedly in recent decades. The number of home-schooled children grew from just a few thousand in the early 1970s to 1.1 million in 2003, having increased 30% between 1999 and 2003 (Penn, 2007).

In 2000, only 52 percent of colleges had formal admission policies for home-schooled students, but by 2005 85% did, in that year a study showing that home-schooled students scored 81 points higher than the national average on the SAT (Penn, 2007).

Though home-schooled children were only 2% of school-age children, they were 12% of the students in the National Spelling Bee and in three out of seven years a home-schooled child won the National Geography Bee (Penn, 2007).

In 2001, a home-schooled boy from Montana completed high school at 15. Not feeling ready for college, he wrote the novel *Eragon* which become a best-seller and was released as a movie in 2006 (Penn, 2007).

Certainly, therefore, children taught well at both home and school should do better!

The author remembers a little rainy Sunday afternoon home instruction and thus, for example, being able to count to 100 at age 4. By age 9 and in grade 4 he was equal top of the class in arithmetic and did fairly well thereafter, finishing school and his first degree with first class honours.

He also remembers going to an expensive private school where there was far too much emphasis on extra-curricular activities, in part to impress upon the parents that they were getting their money's worth, but that he would have preferred more freedom to develop his own lifestyle.

In addition, as always at school, if not University, there is total reliance on rote learning of standard academic material, and little or no instruction on life skills, for example how to deal with such issues as sex, bullying, smoking, and booze (to which list one would now add drugs, of course).

Teenagers should also be taught how to decide as soon as possible upon a realistically achievable career goal and advised on how to achieve it. They should also be instructed how to survive in the workplace, for example how to deal with bullying workmates or bosses.

IQ building

Measurable intelligence or IQ becomes meaningful by the age of four so that before that some effort should be made to 'build IQ' to give the child a head start.

The subject of IQ is sometimes controversial, particularly concerning differences in racial intelligence, but most experts consider that socioeconomic and cultural disadvantages are the main cause of any such differences.

Opinions also differ on what IQ tests really measure, some believing that they simply provide a measure of prior education. Binet, however, originally devised his classical test to measure the causes of learning retardation in public school pupils with a view to providing special classes for slow learners.

To help ensure that young children get a head start some conscious attempt should be made to 'build' their IQ at the age of three, if not before.

Most parents are well meaning and, at the outset at least, many imagine what prodigies their children perhaps are.

The very same parents, however, are those most likely to spoil the child with generosity and he or she may become a stubborn child and a less than good learner because of it.

It is for that reason that input from other parents, for example in play groups, and from professionals, for example in kindergartens, is important.

As for building IQ, the present author believes one obvious step that can be taken is to note the questions in typical IQ tests, for example the Weschler Preschool and Primary Scale of Intelligence (WPPSI), example questions for which can easily be found on the Internet.

Then care can be taken to ensure that the child is taught the simple object identification and number and word recognition exercises it should be capable of at age three.

In case I am thought a hard task master in talking of IQ tests with 3-year-olds, here are a few examples of questions from Binet's intelligence test:

How old are you?
What are the names of these four colours?
Hand me five blocks from that pile.
What is the opposite of the word large?
Which one of these objects is different from the rest?
Point to your nose?

Figure 24.2 shows an example Weschler Preschool and Primary Scale of Intelligence question.

These are none too hard and the point is that a teacher can devise their own test and, as Binet set as a criterion, if on average students in the class can answer 75% of the questions, the test is representative of the norm for that age group, locally at least.

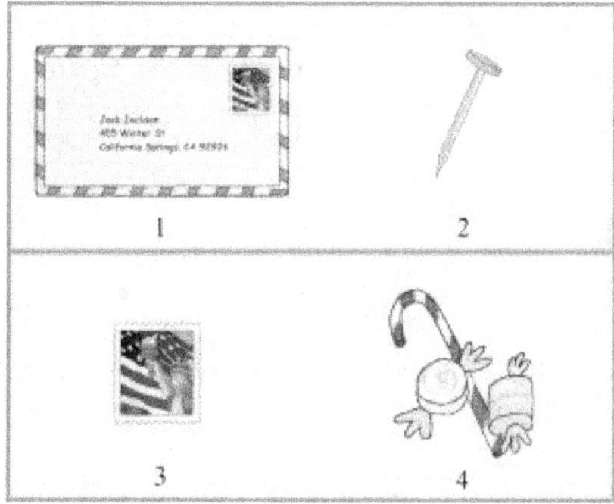

Figure 24.2. Pre-K to Kindergarten WPPSI question:
Which two pictures show the same thing?
{I have improved/simplified the original question. GAM]

As Weiss and Mann (1978) put it: *A person's (or a population's) IQ measures the ability to take IQ tests; it does not measure intelligence.*

Be that as it may, IQ tests do provide some measurement of level of learning and it is vitally important to ensure that the young child does not start school at a disadvantage.

Whether they measure learning or intelligence, or perhaps both, IQ test results generally correspond fairly well with the academic performance of children at school.

Note too that separate IQ tests are available for verbal, spatial, and numerical ability and these tell more about an individual than just a single IQ score.

Therefore, any small learning difficulty identified by an early IQ test can probably be remedied quickly, avoiding much greater difficulties further down the educational track.

In addition, such tests provide an opportunity to observe other aspects of performance such as motivation, persistence or maladaptive behaviours.

Remember also the vivid example given earlier in the chapter of Krech's rats with an enriched environment being found to have developed larger cerebral cortexes, a result which strongly supports Weiss and Mann's view (1978):

Even if we assume that IQ tests measure something like intelligence, we have to recognize that, like many other variable traits, intelligence is very much influenced by the environment.

There is a strong incentive, therefore, for parents to ensure that a child has at least a modestly endowed personal learning centre.

When there is more than one child in the family, of course, sharing of educational resources and experiences should be encouraged, especially when the children are of similar ages.

Nutritional supplements to improve IQ

Dr A.C. Kubala et. al. divided 351 students into two groups, those with higher, and those with lower vitamin C levels. Those with higher C levels were 4.5 points higher in IQ (Holford, 2009).

In another study, Patrick Holford, Stephen Schoenhaler, John Yudkin, Hans Eysenck and Linus Pauling gave 30 children a special multivitamin and mineral supplement and 30 others a placebo. After 8 months the supplement children's average non-verbal IQ[3] was 10 points higher, with some children being up to 20 points higher. Several other studies have had similar findings.

Another study of 200 teenagers in Dakota found that 20 mg (but not 10mg, the RDI being 7 mg) of zinc increased memory accuracy and attention spans (Holford & Colson, 2008).

---

[3] Non-verbal IQ is more fluid and susceptible to brain chemistry, while verbal IQ is more influenced by teaching.

Contrastingly, MIT researchers found that children with diets high in refined carbohydrates such as sugar, white bread and sweets, had IQ up to 25 points lower (Schauss, 1983).

Some of the studies that have made such findings have sometimes included infants, improved IQ from diet improvements showing up a few years down the track. Thus, pregnant women would be wise to ensure that their diets are as healthy as possible and include key nutrients such as the omega essential oils, B-complex, C, and zinc (Holford & Colson, 2008).

Conclusion

Children's brains develop most rapidly in the earliest years and maximum advantage should be taken of this by teaching them as much as possible at home.

To that end a child should have a personal learning centre reflective of the Montessori tradition and both parents should take part in routine educational sessions.

In these it is best to encourage and teach a child to rise above the expected level of learning for their age by, for example, teaching them simple addition at an early age.

In addition, it is best to have the child join learning groups at least occasionally, perhaps run by an educator trained for the purpose. Failing that, friends and neighbours with children of the same age group can be found to help run regular 'play and learn' sessions.

Finally, note that sound diet and appropriate supplementation can also help increase IQ.

24. Making Your Children Smarter

Chapter 25

CONCLUSIONS

*So, decide early on: "If we ever run into problems
that we can't seem to sort out, we will phone a counselor,
visit the pastor, get a referral, speak to trusted friends . . .
so we will do something because we are
committed to one another and have decided that
our marriage deserves all the help it can get.*
Philip Baker, *Decisions of Daring Achievers* (2004).

*Peace is no more than a dream
as long as we need the comfort of the clan.*
Peter Nicols, *Independent,* London, 1 Sept. 1990.

The War of the Sexes

Some feminists claim that women's oppression was the first, most widespread and deepest social wrong in mankind's sorry history, one involving unpaid domestic slavery in marriage or lowly paid domestic slavery to the rich, the latter often having a racial basis.

The war of the sexes is taking a great toll and at present 40 per cent of first marriages and 60 per cent of second marriages end in divorce in the decadent West.

I would argue that much of this is the result of competitive, even confrontational, attitudes encouraged by the Feb Lib movement. Indeed, Tong (1998) notes that: some liberal feminists are sometimes criticized "for being too eager to adopt 'male' values." Despite this, she notes that "de facto gender discrimination lingers."

25. Conclusions

Vive la difference

I believe that we should appreciate, value, and make the best use we can of the differences between the sexes.

Just as the world's different peoples prefer to remember their different histories and cultures, so too should men and women value their different physical, emotional, and perhaps intellectual capabilities. In large part, of course, these arise from girls and boys being brought up somewhat differently to reflect the different roles traditionally associated with them by society.

Overall, these differences result from both *nature* and *nurture* and men and women should learn to make use of these differences in a positive way, rather than viewing them as a question of opposite values and thus potential conflict. As Kipnis (2007) writes:

Plan B: Demand respect for women's inherent differences from men, for our nurturing capacities, out innate moral compass, our emotional intuitiveness, our built-in process oriented . . . you know . . . process. Women's power inheres in our bodies, our childbearing capabilities, our female sensuality – all of which deeply terrify men and society.

The first few lines of that statement are OK, but unfortunately it then degenerates into drivel as feminist writing almost invariably does.

To at least reduce the cultural divide between men and women they should at least understand and be sympathetic to the values of the opposite sex.

For example, women, of course, are more interested in children than men are, and men should understand this and, within reason, be supportive.

Men, on the other hand, have historically often had to work long hours in demanding and sometimes dangerous jobs to support their families.

In these traditional scenarios both sides receive little thanks for their roles and therein lies part of the commonest problem in marriage, one that arises largely from a lack of communication and respect.

In marriage, as well as in courtship, there is little or no meaningful communication. If you eavesdrop on a couple that has been married for a decade or two, you will find the dialogue at all times entirely trivial, for example: "Do we need milk?," in modern times this being said as often as not over a mobile phone while one partner is in the supermarket. I have, therefore, tried to suggest better marital communication habits in Chapter 23.

As for the increasing role women now play in management and politics, Mary Beard sensibly advocates that powerful women should "resist being packaged into a male template" (Beard, 2017).

Decadence

Our societies are becoming meaner, nastier and more violent at an alarming rate. Violence is on the increase everywhere to the point that at which many people don't feel safe on the streets at night and, of course, there is no shortage of street crime during the day as well.

Experiments with rats show that when they are housed beyond a certain population density they begin to fight each other. Evidently humans do the same and we are now accustomed to associating crime and violence with big cities like Chicago and New York.

Increasing numbers of us are addicted to booze, illegal so-called 'party drugs,' as well as prescription drugs like Valium for anxiety, Ritalin for ADHD, and lithium for bipolar disorder (formerly called manic depression).

The ghastly music that young and not so young listen to and gyrate all night too mindlessly boozed and/or drugged in discos is another indicator of social decay. The manic pop groups of today dress and sing atrociously and leap about like primitive loonies.

The bottom line is that you can see the writing on the walls, that is the graffiti that covers much of our miserable megacities, a sure sign that we are regressing back to grunting cave men once again.

Amongst the most disturbing indications of the corruption and decadence in our society are the all too frequent reports of sexual abuse of children by priests, teachers and relatives. It seems that even the once most trusted people in our society can't be trusted any longer.

Sex is ubiquitous in our increasingly depraved society. Brothels were once illegal back street affairs. Now they are advertised in free local newspapers which children collect from the letterbox after coming home from school.

A fundamental change is that homosexuality is on the increase. Once a trait one had to keep secret it is now rampantly displayed at gay Mardi Gras festivals, at gay bars in major cities, and in late night TV ads for homosexual dating services.

Some claim that homosexuality is inherited and a study of 113 people in 33 families in which at least two brothers were homosexual found a genetic marker on the X-chromosome (Xq28) that had a very high correlation with sexual orientation (Galton, 2001).

Genes may play a minor 'predisposory' role but, largely, homosexuality is a learnt behaviour. Typically, for example, the normal heterosexual male has one or two homosexual experiences in adolescence (Robertson, 1981), and no doubt the same applies to women.

Those who become homosexuals, therefore, presumably do so as a result of adopting these early homosexual experiences as an alternative behaviour model.

If alcoholism is to be regarded as a psychiatric illness, as it often is (Davies, 1971), then in my view homosexuality is even more obviously a treatable psychiatric condition.

That said, most of our heterosexual behaviours are also learnt ones, many of them hardly natural or healthy. An example might be what was called 'French kissing' in my youth, that is what can be described as 'tongue kissing', a truly revolting and unhealthy practice like most sexual practices.

The bottom line, sadly, of the increasing corruption, violence, sex, crime, drugs etcetera in our societies is that our intelligence is decreasing and we are in *reverse evolution* (Mohr, 2012a; Mohr & Fear, 2016; Mohr et al., 2018a) and this we should be more concerned about rather than encouraging further division and conflict in our societies as feminist extremists do.

Economic woes and globalization

Thanks largely to our excessive population, but also to incompetent economists and governments, the economies of several countries are in dire straits.

For decades we have undergone cycles of increasing interest rates to supposedly reduce inflation. As Vernon's equations for the Liquid Money Supply and Interest Sensitive Expenditure curves show (Vernon, 1980), however, this has usually increased inflation gradually (Mohr, 2012c, 2014b), resulting in an economic recession every few years that requires a large drop in interest rates to prevent an economic crisis.

Worse still, globalization and the greed of transnational companies has kick-started unstoppable industrial revolutions in Asia, particularly China and India, leaving the US, UK and much of Europe heavily indebted and with their manufacturing sectors largely obliterated.

The result has been acceptance of 5% unemployment rates as "good" in the decaying West, along with bullshit such as Australian Prime Minister Keating's talk of "the clever country" in encouraging people to study often useless University courses to keep them out of the dole queues for a while.

The decline in manufacturing in the West has mainly put men out of work, of course, whilst in Australia more women than men now study at University.

The result has been that, as noted in Chapters 14 to 17, women have taken over most of the education sector and are making increasing inroads into management and politics.

The feminist movement

Having gained the vote long ago, and equal pay, at least in principle, decades ago, the women's movement has made great strides. Nevertheless, Caro and Fox (2008) complain:

Many of the women in our generation find it puzzling that feminism, which promised so much, appears to have stalled. It seemed so logical that, as night followed day, the education of women would mean their passage into all the realms where once only men had wielded power. It seems remarkably clueless now, but when we were hitting our twenties, we truly thought the battles would be long fought and won by the time we retired. What could hold us back if we had degrees in one hand and a job contract in the other? Well, the rest, they say, is history. Turns out quite a lot of things were hanging on our coat tails, and inevitably they included pots, brooms and babies, while up ahead was a glass ceiling protecting a steel floor. Or as a US feminist Laura Liswood once said to Catherine, there's no such thing as the glass ceiling, just a thick layer of men.

Again we have here a feminist 'rave' quickly deteriorating into absurdity and finally objecting to men being in the workplace, albeit in management, at all. Such objections do, indeed, justify the bastard title of this book.

Whilst men who lose their job when circa 40 often have great difficulty ever finding another, women are usually able to obtain employment when they have taken long periods out of the workforce looking after children, presumably because they can be *assumed* to have had a responsible, if not important, role, irrespective of how incompetently it may have been carried out.

Despite this, Caro and Fox (2008) complain:

Financial analysts are only too aware that within the next few decades many women will be facing a financial crisis in retirement. The initial compulsory superannuation legislation failed to take into account the very different shape of women's working lives.

As a result many women now in their fifties, having taken years out of the paid workforce to have and raise children, have painfully small amounts in their super. Citibank research in 2007 backs this up:

➤ *43% of retired Australian women aged 55+ wish they had started saving earlier for retirement.*
➤ *The average monthly income for these women is $1,653 and for men is $2,455.*
➤ *56% of retired women aged 55+ say the pension is their primary source of income compared with 38% of men.*
➤ *Almost half a million retired women (25%) aged 55+ years haven't started saving at all.*
➤ *36% of retired women wish they had done more financial planning.*

The problem here largely relates to women who have been divorced for, if they still had a husband who had worked all through the marriage, then the couple should have had the opportunity to save enough for a comfortable retirement.

Again, therefore, it is the disputative attitude of feminists coming to the fray here, and it is this which has contributed greatly to the high divorce rates at the root of the problem, one which has been exacerbated by the decline in share markets since the GFC (global financial crisis of 2008) which has eroded the retirement savings of most people.

The contact hypothesis

Forbes (1977) proposed that ethnocentricity of different ethnic groups tended to be increased by cultural differences and (presumed negative) contact between them, expressing the ethnocentrism within two groups A and B as:

$$E_a = a_1 \, C(T) \, D(T)$$

$$E_b = b_1 \, C(T) \, D(T)$$

where a_1 and b_1 are assumed to be positive, and are measures of the latent tendency of each group to respond ethnocentrically to each other, C(T) is the amount of contact between the two groups at time T and D(T) is the magnitude of the cultural differences between the two groups at time T.

He further proposed that the amount of contact and the cultural differences between the groups depended upon their proximity, incentives for contact such as trade, and upon the ethnocentrism of the groups, expressing this as:

$$C(T+1) = C(T) (1 + G)/(1 + a_2E_a + b_2E_b)$$

$$D(T+1) = D(T) (1 + a_3E_a + b_3E_b)/[1 + HC(T)]$$

where G is a factor that represents all the factors that determine growth or decline in contact other than the repulsive ethnocentrism and cultural differences of the two groups.

In the last pair of equations ethnocentricity decreases contact and increases cultural differences, as might be expected.

The denominator of the last equation ensures that cultural differences are reduced by contact so long as H is positive (the normal situation).

Contact hypothesis emphasizes that attitude changes with contact or, in general, information transfer, but Forbes assumes that this contact is 'negative.'

If contact is 'positive', as one should hope and aim for, then the ethnocentricity equations can be modified to reflect this by writing them in the form:

$$E_a(T+1) = E_a(T) - a_1 C(T) + a_4 D(T)$$

for ethnocentrism in group A at time T+1, where a_1 and a_4 are positive (Mohr, 2014).

This has obvious application to the War of the Sexes because feminism generally views the differences between men and women in a negative fashion, corresponding to the D term in the last equation, and encourages negative and combative attitudes towards men, corresponding to a plus sign before the C term in the last equation.

If, however, contact was 'positive' and our attitude was *vive la difference*, then 'ethnocentricity' between the sexes would be decreased by a negative sign before both the C and D terms on the right hand side of the last equation.

Mere exposure research

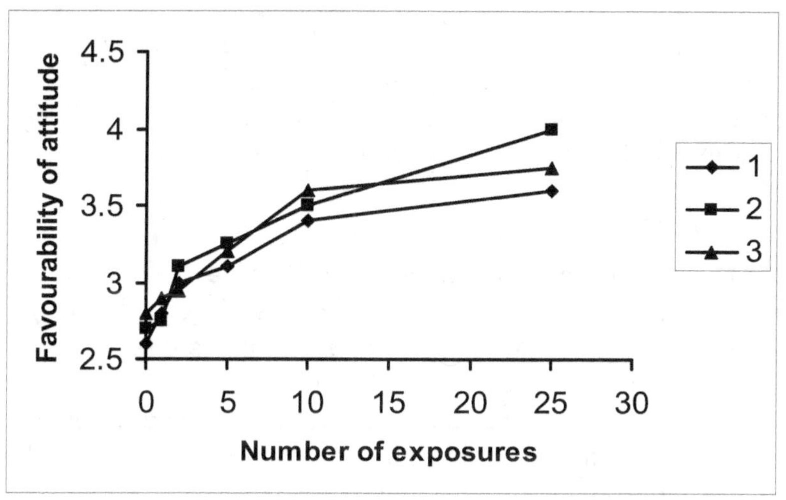

Figure 25.1. Increase in attitude favourability with increasing number of exposures to: 1. Turkish nonsense words. 2. Chinese-like characters. 3. Photographs.

Persuasion studies on message repetition usually focus on the effects of repeated exposure to *information* about attitude objects. In a classic monograph Zajonc (Eagly & Chaiken, 1993) dealt merely with the objects themselves. Figure 25.1 illustrates the increase in attitude favourability with repeated exposure to three types of stimuli, showing a somewhat asymptotic behaviour similar to that of learning curves.

This result is comparable to the 'set size effect' when increasing response is seen with increasing amounts of information, albeit repetition of the same information in the case of mere exposure.

Implications of mere exposure in the War of the Sexes are obvious, principally that people grow accustomed to new and perhaps difficult at first subjects such as sex, if not blasé about them, given time and repeated exposure to them.

The latter observations might remind us that with repeated exposure we become accustomed to, if not hardened to, 'bad things' in life.

In relation to contact hypothesis, of course, the results of Figure 25.1 suggest that, indeed, with more 'exposure from a distance' (but not physical contact) our attitudes towards the opposite sex should become more tolerant, corresponding to the C term in the last equation of the preceding section.

Conclusions

The feminist movement has been active for a long time and the War of The Sexes has involved many battles, for example those over the right to vote and those over equal pay for equal work.

The battle continues and has broken 'the glass ceiling' in many places with increasing numbers of women entering high levels in management and politics.

This book is an attempt to view the War of The Sexes from the male side and thus see the point of view of the casualties of it, almost invariably men.

With the original Industrial Revolution many millions of men lost their jobs in the textile industry. In the last hundred years many more millions lost their jobs in agriculture. More recently many millions more in the West have lost their jobs in the manufacturing industries to cheap labour in Asia.

In the clothing industry, for example, most of the cheap labour is women, often young Chinese women who live six to a room, for example. Sometimes, as once in the mines, child labour has been used, for example for hand-stitching Australian Rules footballs in Asia.

Now men are losing their jobs to women, often unscrupulous women for whom lying and hysterical exaggeration learnt from early childhood is an effective weapon for fighting men.

As noted in the early chapters, men and women are fundamentally different, for example, men cannot bear children.

As noted in Chapter 5, the Gaussian distribution of intelligence is wider for men than for women, doing much to explain the preponderance of men in the mankind's rich history of discovery and innovation.

That men are seemingly more aggressive, whether innately so or because of how they are traditionally brought up (in fact, probably both), has, I believe, contributed to this history. From personal experience I know all too well that to make progress in the more difficult areas of modern science such as the Finite Element Method (Mohr, 1992) or Medicine (Mohr, 2012b, 2013, 2015, 2018c) requires not only reasonable intelligence (and thence intelligent reasoning), but also the capacity to work with great persistence and, sometimes at least, with great intensity.

On the latter point I recall buying a book on raising "gifted" children while doing my PhD in Cambridge with #1 child and wife in tow. I recall that it said that (intellectually) gifted children when nearing the end of a longish task would accelerate their efforts and finish it rapidly, whereas less 'bright' children would tend to 'run out of steam' and struggle as time spent on the task increased, perhaps eventually giving up on it.

On a contrasting note, to quote Caro and Fox (2008) again:

Women's dependence on their sexual attractiveness frightens us, because we recognize its importance
but also understand it is accidental – the result of good genes rather than good management – and temporary.
Like the athlete, the beautiful woman has a short shelf life.

Better than average intelligence also comes from good genes and, I would contend, that it is far less well appreciated than is beauty. Indeed, we seem more inclined to disparage it, for example by calling clever people 'nerds', a term usually associated with men.[4]

From Isaac Newton being ridiculed publicly by cartoons of an apple falling on his head, to more than necessary notice of Einstein once wearing odd socks in public, bullying of those who are different by way of being clever is now epidemic in our schools and society.

In contrast, we deify beautiful young women even though we are fully aware that they are more likely to be spoilt 'bitches' underneath that smiling exterior that some are highly paid for.

Now, with the human population greatly excessive and imperiling our prospects of long term survival (Mohr, 2012c), I would argue that we need, as Cipolla (1974) urged, to breed less and aim for "quality, not quantity" in doing so. If the result is more 'beautiful people', along with more intelligent ones, that would be a good outcome.

Whether they are male or female is of less importance and, no doubt, there will always be approximately equal numbers of both.

Such a division is, given that both sides are given voice, a good application of Mohr's law of politics insofar as, of course, both sides will generally vote largely on a gender basis when possible.

I fear, however, that the predominant issue is that of overpopulation, and thence problems such as resource depletion, pollution, desertification, global warming, extinction of animal species, and evolution of new diseases. Indeed, the result may well be our own extinction (Mohr, 2012c).

---

[4] According to the Macquarie Dictionary a nerd is an idiot or fool. According to the Merriam-Webster Collegiate Dictionary a nerd is an unstylish, unattractive, or socially inept person, especially one slavishly devoted to intellectual or academic pursuits.

Along the way to that sad end there will, of course, be increasing social strife, terrorism, and war, and no doubt the War of The Sexes will continue unabated. I have attempted to suggest some remedies for it in later chapters of this book, whilst I have suggested remedies for the many other problems now facing the human race in the recent books *The Doomsday Calculation* and *The Population Explosion.*

Thus I hope that many a reader perplexed or just intrigued by the War of the Sexes will find useful ideas in this book that may be of help in their own lives.

For example, the sections on the Contact Hypothesis and Mere Exposure Research in this chapter show that with favourable attitude (and thus less 'ethnocentricity') and positive contacts the War of the Sexes could be ended, as could the countless ethnic conflicts ongoing in the world today.

As for the problem of rampant capitalism in several Western nations for several decades, Marxist feminist Evelyn Reed concluded:

The woman question can only be resolved thought the lineup of working men and women against the ruling men and women. This means that the interests of the workers as a 'class' are identical, and not the interests of women as a sex (Reed et al., circa 1970).

The bottom line here, of course, is that on most political and social issues it is best if we overcome potential divisions in society such as sex and wealth, and work together to try and achieve a fairer, generally more prosperous, and happier society.

 ☺☺☺☺☺ **THE END** ☺☺☺☺☺

25. Conclusions

BIBLIOGRAPHY

Atrens D, Curthoys I, *The Neurosciences and Behaviour: An Introduction,* 2nd edn, Academic Press, Sydney (1982).

Baker P, *Decisions of Daring Achievers, Inside Out,* Perth (2004).

Barret, Judith (ed.), *Female Erasure: What You Need To Know About Gender Politics' War on Women, the Female Sex and Human Rights,* Amazon, October 2016.

Beard, Mary, *Women and Power: A Manifesto,* Profile Books, London (2017).

Blundell N, *The World's Greatest Crooks & Conmen, and other mischievous malefactors,* Octopus Books, London (1982).

Bradley RH, Caldwell BM, Early home environment and mental test performance in children from 6 to 36 months, *Development Psychology* 12 (1967) 93-97.

Brando M, Lindsey R, *Brando,* Century, London (1994).

Bryson V, *Feminist Political Theory,* MacMillan, London (1992).

Burt C, The distribution of intelligence, *British Journal of Psychology* 48 (161-174) 1957.

Caro J, Fox C, *The F Word, How we learned to swear by feminism,* New South/UNSW Press, Sydney (2008).

Carter P, *IQ and Psychometric Tests* 2nd edn, Kogan Page, London (2007).

Chodoff P, Lyons H, Hysteria and the hysterical personality, *Am. J. Psychiatry* 114 (1958) 734-40.

Cipolla, CM, *The Economic History of World Population*, 6th edn, Penguin, London (1974).

Crawford R, *But Wait, There's More, A History of Australian Advertising*, Melbourne University Press (2008).

Davies B, *An Introduction to Clinical Psychiatry*, Melbourne University Press, Melbourne (1971).

Eagly AH, Chaiken S, *The Psychology of Attitudes*, Harcourt Brace Jovanovich, Orlando FL (1993).

Fancher RE, *The Intelligence Men: Makers of the IQ Controversy*, WW Norton, New York (1985).

Forbes HD, *Ethnic Conflict: Commerce, Culture, and the Contact Hypothesis*, Yale University Press, New Haven (1997).

Foss, DJ, Hakes, DT, *Psycholinguistics, An Introduction to the Psychology of Language*, Prentice-Hall, Englewood-Cliffs NJ (1978).

Galton D, *In Our Own Image, Eugenics and the Genetic Modification of People*, Little Brown & Co, London (2001).

Greer, Germaine, *The Female Eunuch* (1970). Reprinted by Farrar, Straus & Geraux, New York (2001).

Greer, Germaine, *The Whole Woman*, Doubleday, London (1999).

Harlow HF, The heterosexual affection system in monkeys, *American Psychologist* 17, 1-9 (1962).

Hawking, S, *A Brief History of Time, From The Big Bang to Black Holes*, Bantam/Transworld, London (1989).

Hilgard ER, Atkinson RC, Atkinson RL, *Introduction to Psychology*, 6th edition, Harcourt Brace Jovanovich, New York (1975).

Holford C, Colson D, *Optimum Nutrition For Your Child*, Piatkus, London (2008).

Jencks C, Smith M, Acland H, Bane MJ, Cohen D, Gintis H, Heyns B, Michelson S, *Inequality: A Reassessment of the Effect of Family and Schooling in America*, Penguin, Harmondsworth (1975).

Kinsey AC, Pomeroy WB, Martin CE, Gebhard PH, *Sexual Behaviour in the Human Female*, Saunders, Philadelphia (1948).

Kipnis, Laura, *The Female Thing. Dirt, Sex, Envy, Vulnerability.* Serpent's Tail, London (2007).

Lewis R, *The Bumper Book of Fads and Crazes*, Atlantic Books, London (2005).

Levy A, *Female Chauvinist Pigs, Women and the Rise of Raunch Culture*, Scwartz Publishing, Melbourne (2005).

Likert R, *New Patterns of Management*, McGraw-Hill, New York (1961).

Lindzey G, Hall CS, Thompson RF, *Psychology*, 2nd edn, Worth, New York (1978).

Lynne R, Vanhanen T, *IQ and The Wealth of Nations*, Praeger, Westport CT (2002).

McCormack MH, *What They Don't Teach You at Harvard Business School*, Fontana/Collins, London (1986).

Mohr GA, *The Finite Element Method for Solids, Fluids, and Optimization*, Oxford University Press, Oxford (1992).

Mohr GA, *The Pretentious Persuaders, A Brief History & Science of Mass Persuasion*, Horizon Publishing Group, Sydney (2012a, 2014).

Mohr GA, *Curing Cancer & Heart Disease, Proven Ways to Combat Aging, Atherosclerosis, and Cancer*, Xlibris, Sydney (2012b).

Mohr GA, *The Doomsday Calculation, The End of the Human Race*, Xlibris, Sydney (2012c).

Mohr GA, *The War of The Sexes, Women Are Getting On Top,* Xlibris, Sydney (2012d).

Mohr GA, *Heart Disease, Cancer & Aging, Proven Neutraceutical & Lifestyle Solutions,* Horizon Publishing Group, Sydney (2013).

Mohr GA, *The History and Psychology of Human Conflicts,* Horizon Publishing Group, Sydney (2014).

Mohr GA, *Elementary Thinking for the 21st Century,* Xlibris, Sydney (2014b).

Mohr GA, *The 8-Week+ Program to Reverse Cardiovascular Disease,* Book Venture, Ishpeming MI (2015).

Mohr GA, Fear E, *World Religions: The History, The History, Issues, and Truth,* Xlibris, Sydney (2015).

Mohr GA, Fear E, *The Brainwashed, From Consumer Zombies to Islamism & Jihad,* Inspiring Publishers, Canberra (2016).

Mohr GA, *The Population Explosion: The Problems, Solutions, and Predictions,* Amazon-Kindle, Middletown DE (2018).

Mohr, Geoff, *Mohr's Law of Hierarchies, and many other Mohr's Laws,* Amazon-Kindle (2018b).

Mohr GA, *The DIY Cardiovascular Cure, A Comprehensive Program to Reverse Atherosclerosis,* Amazon-Kindle (2018c).

Mohr GA, Mohr RS, Mohr PE, *The Psychology of Hope,* Balboa Press, Bloomington IN (2018a).

Mohr GA, Mohr PE, Mohr RS, *Brainwashed Zombies: Religious, Political & Consumer Persuasion,* Amazon-Kindle (2018b).

Mohr GA, Mohr PE, Mohr RS, *World Religions, From Animism to Mohronism,* Amazon-Kindle, Middletown DE (2018c).

Morgan CT, King RA, Robinson NM, *Introduction to Psychology,* 6th edn, McGraw-Hill, Tokyo (1979).

Odle F, *The Picture Story of British Inventions,* World Distributors, Manchester (1966).

O'Guinn TC, Allen CT, Semenik RJ, *Advertising and Integrated Brand Promotion.* Thomson South-Western, Mason OH (2006).

Ostrander S, Schroeder L, *Superlearning,* Delacorte Press/Confucian Press, New York (1979).

Packard V, *The Waste Makers*, Pelican, Harmondsworth (1963).

Packard V, *The People Shapers,* Nelson, Melbourne (1978).

Penn, *Microtrends, The Small Forces Behind Today's Big Changes*, Allen Lane, London (2007).

Popham WJ, Measurement as an Instructional Catalyst, *Measurement, Technology, and Individuality in Education,* Proc. 1982 Educational Testing Society Invitational Conference, Josey-Bass, San Francisco (1983).

Reed Evelyn, Is Man an "Aggressive Ape", *International Socialist Review,* November 1970, Vol. 31, No. 8, pp. 27-31, 40-42.

Reed E, Hansen J, Waters M-A, *Cosmetics, Fashions, and the Exploitation of Women,* circa 1970.

Robertson I, *Sociology*, 2nd edn, Worth, New York (1981).

Robbins SP, *Management*, 4th edn, Prentice-Hall, Englewood Cliffs NJ (1994).

Sargent M, *Drinking and Alcoholism in Australia: A Power Relations Theory,* Longman Cheshire, Melbourne (1979).

Schauss A G, Nutrition and behaviour, *J App Nutr* 35 (1983) 30-35.

Seitz PFD, *The Maternal Instinct in Animal Subjects*, Annual meeting of the American Psychosomatic Society, New Orleans, 1954.

Skodal M, Skeels HM, A final follow-up study of one hundred adopted children, *Journal of Genetic Psychology* 75 (1949) 85-125.

Sweezy PM, *The Theory of Capitalist Development*, Dennis Dobson, London (1946).

Sykes CJ, *Dumbing Down Our Kids: Why American Children Feel Good About Themselves But Can't Read, Write or Add*, St Martin's Griffin, New York (1995).

Tong RP, *Feminist Thought, A More Comprehensive Introduction*, 2nd edn, Allen & Unwin, Sydney (1998).

Vander AJ, Sherman JH, Luciano DS, *Human Physiology*, 6th edn, McGraw-Hill, New York (1994).

van Lawick-Goodall, Jane, *In the Shadow of Man*, Houghton Mifflin, Boston (1971).

Vernon, Jack, *Macroeconomics* (2nd edn), The Dryden Press, Hinsdale IL (1980).

Vernon PE, *Intelligence and Attainment Tests*, University of London Press, London (1960).

Weiss ML, Mann AE, *Human Biology and Behaviour, An Anthropological Perspective*, 2nd edn, Little Brown, Boston MA (1978).

Wonnacott P, Wonnacott R, *Economics*, McGraw-Hill, New York (1979).

Worsley P, *Introducing Sociology*, Penguin, Harmondsworth (1970).

Wurtzel, Elizabeth, *Bitch, In Praise of Difficult Women*, Quartet Books, London (1998).

THE WAR OF THE SEXES

To restore balance to the issue topics covered include:

- A brief history of the War of the Sexes.
- The usual differences in upbringing for boys & girls.
- The many ability and other differences between the sexes.
- The maternal instinct and teen & single mothers.
- The many ways in which a woman can capture a man.
- Exploitation of women in the consumer society.
- Decadent societies with high divorce rates.
- Women taking over the workforce at the expense of men.
- Women moving into higher management and politics.
- The key reasons for, and solutions to, the increasing decadence and moral and financial bankruptcy in the West.
- Planning relationships, marriage, and children.
- Improving relationships & making your children smarter.
- The contact hypothesis and mere exposure research.

Readers will find many life-improving ideas in this book.

G. A. Mohr did his PhD at Churchill College, Cambridge. He published circa 60 papers for 20 international journals and more than 25 books, including:
A Microcomputer Introduction to the Finite Element Method
Finite Elements for Solids, Fluids, and Optimization
The Pretentious Persuaders, A Brief History & Science of Mass Persuasion
Curing Cancer & Heart Disease,
Proven Ways to Combat Aging, Atherosclerosis & Cancer
The Variant Virus, Introducing Secret Agent Simon Sinclair
The Doomsday Calculation, The End Of The Human Race
Heart Disease, Cancer, & Ageing: Proven Neutraceutical & Lifestyle Solutions
2045: A Remote Town Survives Global Holocaust
The History & Psychology of Human Conflict
Elementary Thinking for the 21st Century
The 8-Week+ Program to Reverse Cardiovascular Disease
The Scientific MBA;   Mohr's Law of Hierarchies;   The DIY Cardiovascular Cure

Also with R.S. Mohr/Richard Sinclair & P.E. Mohr/Edwin Fear:
The Evolving Universe: Relativity, Redshift and Life from Space
World Religions: The History, Psychology, Issues & Truth
World War 3, When & How Will It End?
The Brainwashed, From Consumer Zombies to Islamic Jihad
Human Intelligence, Learning & Behaviour
New Theories of The Universe, Evolution, and Relativity
The Psychology of Hope;   The Population Explosion
Brainwashed Zombies: Religious, Political & Consumer Persuasion